THE SMALL BOAT CERTIFICATION SERIES

TEACHING FUNDAMENTALS FOR SAILING INSTRUCTION

The National Standard for Quality Sailing Instruction

Published by the United States Sailing Association (US Sailing) The non-profit National Governing Body for the Sport of Sailing. This is the third edition of the book originally published in 1995.

©1995 by the United States Sailing Association ©1999 by the United States Sailing Association

© 2012 by the United States Sailing Association

The information offered in this book reflects the cumulative experience of many volunteers involved with sailing. It offers suggestions about how to safely teach sailing (and the operation of a safety" boat for supervision and rescue), but there may be other effective ways as well. It should be understood that the application of all this information should be adapted to each "individual" situation taking into account such factors as the age, size, experience and potential disabilities of each sailor, the type of boat being used, the weather, location, other water activities and, all other factors which may apply. Each person involved with sailing should accept that the sport of sailing and the conduct of any sailing or sailing related program entail and are subject to certain inherent risks, including serious injury.

Printed in the United States of America

United States Sailing Association
15 Maritime Drive
Portsmouth, RI 02871 - 6015

www.ussailing.org

Cover images by Matt Cohen and Justin Chando

ACKNOWLEDGMENTS

US Sailing would like to thank the following contributors to this manual:

Dr. Jeffrey Barsch, EdD, Rich Brew, Megan Buchanan, Brad Dellenbaugh, Dr. Derrick Fries, Ph.D., Pat Giella, John Kantor, Hart Kelley, Jeff Johnson, Felix Kloman, Timmy Larr, Ginny Long, Arn Manella, Laurie O'Brien, Joni Palmer, and Susie Trotman. Many National Faculty members were contributors and creators of the original editions of this book, formerly known as *Teaching and Coaching Fundamentals*. The original text was made possible in part by a generous grant from Sail America. The updated 2012 edition was developed due to the dedication of the following:

Emlie Barkow hails from Pine Lake, WI amongst a large family of sailors. Emlie graduated from Hobart & William Smith Colleges where she sailed and received her teaching certification. Emlie has been Program Director at Pleon Yacht Club, Marblehead MA before her current position of Program Director at Newport Harbor Yacht Club in Balboa, CA.

Morgan Collins is the Executive Director of Sail Sand Point, in Seattle, WA. Currently the Chair of the Community Sailing Council, Morgan is a Level 1 Instructor Trainer, a US Powerboating instructor, and a former recipient of the "Marty Luray Award" which is presented annually to the person who has made an outstanding and unselfish contribution to furthering public access sailing.

Peter Durant is Executive Director of the Community Boating Center in New Bedford, Massachusetts. He has spent 20 years in the marine industry in public and private organizations working to improve access to the water and the experience on it, as well as the standards and instructor training necessary to improve boater safety.

Guy Fleming has been working for Waikiki Yacht Club since 1985 and has ben their Sailing Director since 1991. He was certified as a Level 1 IT and Level 2 CT in 1993 before becoming a Master Instructor Trainer in 1995 Since then he has been certified as a Regional Race Officer, a US Sailing Judge, A Powerboat Instructor, a Basic Keelboat Instructor Trainer and a Level 3 coach.

Stu Gilfillen is the Sailing Programs Administrator at US Sailing. He previously served as the Executive Director of the Sarasota Youth Sailing Program in Sarasota, FL and Sailing Director for both the Edgartown and Beverly Yacht Clubs. Currently the staff liaison to US Sailing's Community Sailing Committee and Committee for Sailors with Disabilities, he is a US Sailing Level 1 Instructor Trainer, a Level 2 coach and a US Powerboating Instructor. Stu also serves as the agenda coordinator for US Sailing's National Sailing Programs Symposium.

Kim Hapgood has served as the Program Director for Sail Newport since 1996. She's a member of the US Sailing Training Committee, co-chair of small boat National Faculty, a Master Instructor Trainer, avid match racer and semi-active judge. She completed her undergraduate work at Brandeis University and her graduate degree in Higher Education Administration at Columbia University. Kim is also a seasonal PT Harbormaster for City of Newport, RI.

Hart Kelley is the Head Sail Training Coach for cadet leadership training in the Coastal Sail Training Program at the US Coast Guard Academy. He is co-chair of the Small Boat National Faculty, Vice-Chair of Standards and Credentials for the Training Committee, a Level 1 Master Instructor Trainer, Level 2 Coach Trainer, Basic Keelboat Instructor Trainer, Keelboat Cruising Instructor Trainer, Powerboat Instructor and speaker at the National Sailing Programs Symposium.

Steve Maddox serves as a US Sailing Small Boat Instructor Trainer and Coach Trainer and US Powerboating Master Instructor Trainer, and as a regional training coordinator for both. He also is the founder and president of SeaAffinity, Inc., a non-profit sailing program in Baltimore, MD.

Rachael Miller is the founder/Director of the Rozalia Project for a Clean Ocean whose mission is to find and remove marine debris using remotely operated vehicles, sonar, and nets from aboard *American Promise,* a Ted Hood 60'. She is a member of the US Sailing National Faculty and Training Committee as well as a Level 1 and 2 Instructor Trainer. Rachael raced Lasers, Europe Dinghies, J24s and was a member of the Brown University Sailing Team. She is a certified windsurfing, kitesurfing and snowkiting instructor.

Deb Sullivan-Gravelle grew up in Boulder, Colorado. After college she moved to Seattle, where she was introduced to sailing and never looked back. One of the co-founders of Sail Sand Point in Seattle, Deb spent 4 years running the Bermuda Sailing Association before returning to Colorado. She is a Level 1 Instructor Trainer and Level 2 Coach Trainer, a member of the National Faculty and former co-organizer for the National Sailing Programs Symposium.

Table of Contents

Introduction

Welcome to the world of teaching sailing! You will find it quite different from being a sailor or a student. It can be challenging and demanding, but you will receive a great amount of satisfaction from teaching others how to sail.

Teaching beginners is a great challenge with an even greater reward. Beginning sailors learn a huge volume in a very short time. . Students progress from never having seen a sailboat, then the next week they are sailing it by themselves, largely because of quality instruction. Just like learning the ABC's is the foundation of learning language, learning proper skills as a beginning sailor is the foundation they will use for the rest of their sailing careers.

US Sailing's Training Philosophy

US Sailing sets high standards for both instructors and students. Instructors are to teach more than basic sailing skills, and should strive to instill:

- a sense of good seamanship,
- proper attitude for self and others,
- a love for sailing,
- a commitment to learning,
- and stewardship of the environment.

To facilitate this instruction, US Sailing has developed a training philosophy. The four cornerstones of this philosophy are:

1. "Students First, Instructors Second"
   Instructors, coaches and trainers should put the student's needs first and the instructor's goals and expectations second.

2. A Building Block Approach
   Instruction should offer a safe and logical progression from previously learned skills to new ones. The emphasis should be on active on-the-water participation by the student.

3. Balance Student Needs With Student Outcomes
   The teaching methodology needs to take into account that people learn in different ways at different speeds. People also have different reasons for being in a sailing class. To make sailing a successful experience for a student, instructors have to make a conscious effort to balance student needs and expectations with student outcomes.

4. Safety, Fun and Learning
   The learning and teaching process has to emphasize safety, fun and learning while developing safe, confident and responsible sailors.

Small Boat Sailing Level 1 Instructor Course & This Manual

The Small Boat Sailing Level I Instructor Course assumes that candidates are competent sailors and that they have experience in operating a safety boat. The goal of this course is to offer insights on how to teach all kinds of people in a safe environment and to make that process fun.

Teaching Fundamentals for Sailing is a book on the theory of teaching, especially as it applies to sailing. The Small Boat Sailing Level 1 Instructor Guide is a practical way to teach specific lessons to students.

How to Use This Manual

This book is laid out in sections, so you can refer to topics found in one part, with related topics found in another. The pagination begins at 1 in each section so the pages in Section 1 start as 1-1 and the pages in Section 2 start as 2-1.

Section 1 — Instructor Responsibilities discusses the standards, roles and responsibilities of a US Sailing Small Boat Level I Instructor.

Section 2 — Risk Management explains important considerations for avoiding risks or injuries while instructing.

Section 3 — Teaching Theory and Techniques connects the theories of learning, teaching, sports psychology, communication skills and leadership to the practice of everyday sailing instruction. Everyone processes information differently, and effective teaching is not possible without understanding this.

Section 4— Preparing for Instructing offers insight on how to pull together the resources provided to develop thorough, well-planned sailing lessons.

Section 5 — Teaching to Different Audiences offers insight about how to teach different people. Understanding that every individual may need special consideration will make their sailing experience successful.

More about US Sailing

Since 1897 the United States Sailing Association (US Sailing) has provided support for American sailors at all levels of sailing in all kinds of sailboats. US Sailing is a not-for-profit organization and the official National Governing Body of Sailing as designated by the U.S. Congress in the Amateur Sports Act. It has national Training Programs for sailors in dinghies, windsurfers, multihulls, keelboats and powerboats. It is also the official representative to the International Sailing Federation (ISAF).

The primary objective of US Sailing's Training Program is to provide a national standard of quality instruction for all people learning to sail. The US Sailing Certification System includes a series of course books, including *Learn Sailing Right! Beginning Sailing*, a program of student certifications and an extensive educational and training program for instructors. The Certification System is designed to create safe, responsible and confident sailors who meet specific performance and knowledge standards. It's one of the world's most highly developed and effective national training systems for students and sailing instructors, and is recognized nationally and internationally.

Professional Responsibilities of a US Sailing Certified Instructor

As a US Sailing certified sailing instructor, you assume responsibilities that extend well beyond simply giving sailing lessons. As a professional, you are responsible to your students, their parents, your employer and co-workers, US Sailing and yourself. The degree to which you live up to those responsibilities largely determines your level of professionalism.

1. Responsibility to Your Students

Safety

People expect to be safe while in the care of an expert. As a sailing instructor you are the expert. You have a responsibility to safeguard your students from harm. You have a legal duty and a personal responsibility to try to anticipate danger and protect them from it. You are responsible for taking charge of all facets of the learning environment and maintaining sufficient control of it so that nobody gets hurt.

If a student becomes injured, you have a duty to provide care to the extent of your training. More extensive treatment, beyond what you are trained to do, should be administered by qualified medical personnel.

Fun

Whatever style of sailing your various students aspire to (cruising, daysailing, racing, windsurfing, etc.), one thing they have in common is a desire for recreation. Sailing long ago lost its commercial value as a cost-effective mode of transportation. Today people sail for fun. One of the first and most common questions friends and family ask after class is, "Was it fun?" You, the instructor, have to deliver that reward or risk losing your students. If you lose your students, you are out of work, and they are out of a good learning opportunity.

> **INSTRUCTORS TAKE NOTE...**
>
> Safety, fun and learning are the three major directives for every sailing instructor. If your students enjoy themselves, return uninjured, and learn something new and interesting you will have met your primary responsibilities to your students.

Learning

Much of this manual is devoted to the specifics of teaching and learning sailing. You succeed when your students learn. But your success in getting through to them depends on setting the right tone from the outset of your relationship.

Students naturally expect a certain degree of personal attention and care from their instructor in helping them learn. No one likes feeling anonymous or neglected. Start by memorizing students' names or use name tags to help break the ice and begin team building. Avoid the appearance of playing favorites by trying to meet the needs of ALL students. Take a few moments to make contact with each individual in your care and continue to give feedback to each of your students, as it is an important element in trust building and leadership.

Finally, treat your students with respect:

- Arrive for class on time and prepared.
- Give the class your undivided attention.
- Greet each student as you would a guest.

- Be polite and courteous at all times.
- Protect their personal confidences with proper discretion
- Accept your students' differences objectively and professionally. It is inappropriate to be judgmental.
- Never mock or make fun of a student in or out of class.
- Provide all students with ample individual supervision.
- Answer their questions thoughtfully.
- Follow-up on any promises you make.

Sailing students want to have FUN. They expect to be SAFE. They hope to LEARN. Be the professional that fulfills their expectation.

Recognizing Sexual Abuse

If a kid tells an adult that he or she has been sexually abused, the adult may feel uncomfortable and not know what to say or do. At a minimum, offer the kid protection and take action to stop the abuse. Although laws vary from one state to another, the proper authorities, such as the local Protection Agency, the Police or the District Attorney's office **must** be notified of any concerns of abuse. Here are some recommendations for appropriate touch:

- **Avoid situations where you are isolated and one on one with a student.** Always be in view of others. If someone misinterprets your actions, it is his or her word against yours.
- **Don't initiate physical contact.** But if, for example, a kid initiates a hug, then it is appropriate to respond in kind.
- **Play it safe.** What you may consider a helpful act, such as putting sunscreen on a student's back, may make that adult or kid feel uncomfortable or sexually violated. An innocent gesture can be misinterpreted!
- **Use good judgment.** Be aware of personal space and interactions and act upon any suspected or known physical or sexual abuse.

Recognizing Physical Abuse

The statistics on physical abuse are alarming. Of the estimated hundreds of thousands of victims battered each year, thousands die. For those who survive, the emotional trauma remains long after the external bruises have healed. Communities and courts have recognized that these emotional "hidden bruises" can be treated. Students who have been abused may display:

- Poor self-image
- Inability to rely on or trust others
- Aggressive and disruptive behavior
- Passive or withdrawn behavior
- School or job failures
- Alcohol or drug abuse

Battering is not the only kind of abuse. Many students are victims of neglect, sexual abuse, and emotional abuse.

Parents in a Junior Sailing Program

One of the biggest questions program organizers and instructors have to address is the degree of parent involvement in a sailing program. Sailing is a participation sport. Unlike spectator sports, such as football and baseball, opportunities and infrastructure for spectators in sailing events are limited. Many of your student's parents are new to sailing and need assistance in understanding what their kids are doing and how they can support them. Other might be experts in the sport and need to be directed in their involvement working with the instructors. Parents are every bit as much a customer as their kids and deserve appropriate respect and courtesy. Successful programs find a way to listen to, include, and respond to parents.

A Customer Service Mentality

The best way to work with parents is to think of them as customers. This doesn't mean you have to adhere to the old slogan that "the customer is always right," but that it is better to have healthy relationships with parents so they remain customers of the program. Over the duration of a season, Instructors can expect to deal with helpful parents, curious parents, intrusive parents and irate parents. In fact, all of these traits may describe one parent or a variety of parents. The bottom line is that parents want to support their kids the best way they know how. If a parent is left to devise their own method of supporting their kid or kids, parental support may end up in conflict with the goals and methods of the Instructor and the program. Here are a few suggestions to provide parents with a structure to help, rather than hinder a sailing program:

1. Create and then notify parents of the program's **policies**.
2. Create a variety of **parent activities** that support the program and/or a class. **Provide opportunities** for parents to be involved in the program, and give them a voice in curriculum, governances, and programmatic goals.
3. **Report** back to parents on the success of their kids.
4. Inform parents of any **needs** of the program.
5. Create social opportunities to **strengthen relationships** between parents, instructors, program organizers and kids.

Policies

Policies are the rules and guidelines that define how parents, kids, instructors and program organizers will act and interact. Good policies provide **rules and directions for participation**, define the process of **discipline**, lay the groundwork for handling **complaints**, **reduce the risks** to sailors ashore and afloat, identify **roles and responsibilities** and the chain of command, and facilitate good **communication**.

For example, program organizers should develop a policy that permits sailing instructors to teach without outside interference. Within the framework of the instructional program, include parents in specific activities while restricting them from the instructional area.

Some parents may not be happy with such an arrangement. While many parents are accomplished sailors and racers, remind parents that they would not walk into a schoolroom to give the teacher directions. Explain that sailing instructors are employees who have a right to a proper work environment and a responsibility to all of their students. A parent's experience and expertise as a sailor is highly valuable, so find an outlet that allows that parent to contribute. To mitigate parental concerns about the direction of instruction, give them a voice outside of the class. Parental input to the design and development of the entire program can improve the overall program immensely. Finally, the program organizers and instructors must strongly enforce this policy and not tolerate any disruption of the sailing program. Any questions regarding the sailing program can be directed to the Head Instructor or Program Organizers during appropriate times.

Parent Orientation Sessions

It is essential that prior to the start of the program, program organizers call a parent orientation session to review the policies and details of the program. Included in this orientation should be a review of how parents can be involved in the program (parent day, guest speaker, car pools, chaperones, race committee, parent helper-of-the-day, and social activity organizers), the rules for the program, and the disciplinary code. Program organizers and instructors should be frank with parents about their intention to maintain the integrity of a program by dismissing persistent offenders. The orientation should detail student drop-off and pick-up arrangements, emphasizing students must be prompt for class and must be picked up at the correct time. Instructors must not be expected to baby sit class members who are waiting to be picked up.

The professional nature of the program should be stressed, along with the planning that has gone into its development. Organizers should detail the training that instructors have undergone and the usefulness the training will provide in relation to the students, organization, and parents. Parents should be reminded that continued cooperation and support will further the sailing program's success.

Parent Participation and Information Updating

Arrange opportunities throughout the program for parents to participate. These opportunities can include cookouts, displays, and take parents sailing day. In longer programs a mid-season newsletter, written by the students, can provide more information to the parents on program events. In shorter programs "Show What You Know Day" can allow parents a glimpse into the activities at your program. Planned events like these are essential to retain the interest of the parents and also provide the instructors an opportunity to discuss the progress of each student.

For programs running on a shoestring budget with volunteer instructors, it is especially important to discuss the role of parents can play in the program's success, either as helpers or fund raisers.

Involvement of Parents and Students in Program Planning

Regular meetings with parents help to get them working for you and with you. These meetings provide a forum for discussing the sailing program. Ask for the parent's input on the program and any related topics at the end of the season, and invite them to evaluate and improve the program in the off season.

About four to six weeks after the end of the training program, organize a social event for the students. Organize a social event, or show sailing films of the previous season's activities.

Set time aside to ask each of the classes what they liked and disliked about their courses. Collate this information so you can discuss it at the next program organizers' meeting. The program organizers will use this information to prepare a comprehensive program outline (curriculum) for the upcoming season. Once the program organizers have received the students' and parents' input on the program, program planning can be finalized. Program planning should be developed early so proper instructor job descriptions can be prepared to hire the instructional staff next season.

Several weeks before a program starts, all information relating to the upcoming sailing program should be sent out to participants. This is also the time when enrollment takes place. Rather than having parents mail in applications, checks, and indemnity forms, change the registration format so that enrollment is through personal appearance with the students present. This method ensures that both the parents and students understand the nature of the course, including equipment, safety, and swimming ability, etc. The enrollment day should coincide with a function at the program facility to encourage turnout. If this isn't possible, enrollment should be held during a weekend with the sessions at 9 a.m., 1 p.m., and 3 p.m., to ensure that all parents can attend with their kids. Show films and serve refreshments to capture the interest of the participants and establish enthusiasm early in the season. Parents should bring all necessary medical documents, disclaimers, consent forms, as a condition of enrollment.

Just prior to the start of the sailing program, a social evening for students and parents should be held as an ideal method to introduce the sailing instructors. Go over the main points of the program, including any new classes or activities.

2. Responsibility to Your Employer

There is a certain amount of give-and-take in any employer/employee relationship. Your personal objectives in teaching sailing may not necessarily be the same as those of your employer. Ultimately, compatibility depends on both parties understanding and cooperating with one another. If you are a paid instructor, bear in mind who signs the paychecks. To maintain good relations at work you need to be aware of your employer's point of view. You have professional responsibilities to your employer.

What does being Professional mean?

The term professional implies a certain quality of performance. It suggests one who is thorough, effective, dependable, objective, focused, and does a good job. Whether or not you teach sailing as your principal livelihood, your employer probably wants and expects you to be "professional." Being professional should include:

- Teaching effectively and safely
- Abiding by all terms of employment
- Abiding by all laws and regulations
- Keeping required certifications and licenses current
- Abiding by a high standard of ethics
- Being respectful of authority
- Taking your job responsibilities seriously
- Being thoroughly prepared
- Being a dependable and cooperative teammate
- Being a good role model
- Being courteous, tactful and discreet
- Avoiding offensive, discriminatory, or vulgar language and behavior.
- Completing assignments neatly, promptly and correctly
- Being punctual and respectful of others' time
- Accepting responsibility for yourself, your assistants, and your students
- Being respectful of your employer's property
- Neither using nor tolerating alcohol or drugs on the job

Job Descriptions

A job description normally defines an employee's exact duties and areas of responsibility. Most employers put job descriptions in writing. Written job descriptions are required by labor law in some states. In sailing schools where staff members perform more than one job function or occasionally pitch in and help each other, job descriptions help to minimize confusion and misunderstandings. They spell out who is responsible for what, and they specify who is accountable to whom.

If your employer does not supply a written job description, ask for one. Get clarification about anything confusing or unclear. It is helpful to save all memos and correspondence from your employer. This will help you if any misunderstanding ever arises about your duties. You will have your written instructions to guide and support you.

What are my legal responsibilities as an Instructor?

As a sailing instructor you automatically assume certain legal responsibilities and obligations both personally and on behalf of your employer. The most important responsibility is the safety of your students. You have what is legally known as a duty of care. If you fail in that duty, and someone is hurt as a result, you may be deemed negligent. If you are negligent, you and your employer may be found responsible or liable for damages.

If a student is injured while in your care, he or she may seek compensation through the courts and/or your liability insurance coverage. Most reputable employers maintain suitable liability insurance coverage which affords protection for their employees. The type and extent of your employer's coverage, however, may not be sufficient to fully protect you personally from a claim. For your own protection do not fail to thoroughly research the complete extent of your liability exposure and how much insurance protection your employer provides. You may wish to carry a back-up personal "umbrella" liability policy, possibly through your renter's or homeowner's policy.

With proper precautions and supervision most accidents can be avoided.

US Sailing certified instructors are automatically covered by US Sailing with a $10,000,000 liability policy in excess of their employers' insurance. Bear in mind that current CPR, first aid and US Sailing membership are certification requirements. If you allow them to lapse, you risk losing this valuable coverage.

The best way to avoid the entire thorny issue of liability claims, of course, is with accident prevention. The following precautions can serve as guidelines:

- Gain experience and knowledge and teach effectively.
- Plan your lessons carefully in advance.
- Inspect all equipment and surroundings for safety.
- Caution students in advance about potential dangers (e.g., accidental jibes, hair near winches and turning blocks, etc.).
- Avoid decisions that put students into unnecessarily risky situations.
- Closely supervise students. Anticipate their mistakes.
- Train and closely supervise your assistants. You are responsible for their actions and omissions.
- Obey and enforce all rules for safety and rules of conduct for your program. Prominently post rules and charts of any off limits areas.
- Have emergency equipment and first aid supplies on hand and post procedures to follow in an emergency.
- Require students wear life jackets at all times near or on the water.
- Stay alert. Expect the unexpected. Respond appropriately when the unexpected occurs.

When an accident occurs, care for the injured party. Rescuing equipment and gear is always secondary to helping people. After dealing with the injury or accident, follow your organization's reporting procedures. Having the injured person(s) fill-out and sign a standardized accident/incident report form is also recommended. Be sure to write down your own recollection of all the facts of the incident in as full a detail as you can remember. If a claim results, there will certainly be official reports to fill out. All circumstances surrounding the accident will need to be documented to verify the facts of the claim. Those circumstances will determine the degree of negligence and the amount of any liability. At that point routine record keeping can become legal documentation and can carry considerable weight in litigation, which may occur many years later. Completion of accident reports requires serious thought.

What is the Importance of Record Keeping?

Paperwork may seem like drudgery at times, but it is an important and necessary part of an instructor's professional responsibility. Keeping accurate records of your job activity is not only good teaching and business practice; it can provide valuable information in the event of a liability suit.

> Keep files and records well organized so you can find important information in an emergency.

Thorough record keeping which documents responsible job performance can help defend against a negligence claim. Sloppy, sporadic, or incomplete records, on the other hand, may be used to show a pattern of carelessness or indifference. Because your records could end up in court someday, think of them as an opportunity to illustrate your diligence. Legal matters aside, they can also help a substitute instructor pick up where you left off if you become ill or incapacitated, and they help show you as a professional.

Student records should include attendance rosters, skill completion records, notes on individual progress, test scores (if used), a detailed daily log of weather and water conditions, daily lesson plans, comments, waivers, etc. Be sure to note any irregular occurrences such as medical emergencies, unusual behavior, equipment damage, etc. Proper documentation of a student's experience is required for various boating and sailing licenses and certifications.

It is prudent to have a medical card/form on file for each student with information regarding any special medical conditions, allergies, personal physicians, emergency phone numbers, and, if the student is a minor, parental permission for emergency treatment. The card, or a copy of it, should be immediately available to any medical service which takes over responsibility for the student's welfare in a medical emergency.

Regular equipment inspection and maintenance reports are helpful to keep track of the condition of boats and equipment. In a busy program, with sailors coming and going every day, you should not assume everything will remain in good working order. A professional leaves nothing to chance. Every piece of equipment should be inspected daily and anything out of order so noted in the daily inspection report. An inspection report isn't something you fill out only when something is wrong. A clean report, indicating that everything was found to be in good order, can help in defending a later liability claim of faulty equipment or negligent maintenance.

To facilitate inspections it is helpful to arrange equipment storage facilities so that all things alike are together. If designed so that each item has its own separate space, a quick visual check will reveal anything missing or out of order. If you allow equipment to be tossed in a disorderly pile, inspections will take longer and probably will be less thorough.

A properly organized and managed equipment storage scheme is important for convenient access, ease of inspection and maintenance, not to mention a well-kept professional appearance. The mariner's saying, "a place for everything and everything in its place," applies as much to storage ashore as it does aboard boats.

Sexual Harassment

In today's world everyone must be aware of certain sensitivities regarding gender, ethnic origin, disability, age, sexual preference, etc. Instructors must be aware of all these concerns whether they are dealing with adults or kids. They must be aware of, or become aware of, what is considered an appropriate interaction with a student.

It is imperative that instructors learn how to safely and responsibly interact with their supervisors, co-workers and students by increasing their awareness of personal boundaries and personal rights as they relate to discrimination, sexual harassment, and abuse. Instructors are often idolized, and so they need to be careful about their interactions with students.

Instructors must learn how to protect themselves against misinterpretations or allegations of abuse or harassment. Finally, instructors must become aware of their responsibility to take action if they suspect that a student may be a victim of abuse or if a student tells an instructor about being abused.

As an instructor, you are vulnerable to charges of sexual harassment or physical abuse.

3. Responsibility to US Sailing

> Once you become a US Sailing certified instructor, a lot of people will be counting on you.

When US Sailing confers certification to an Instructor, it vouches for that person's training and skill to perform the essential prescribed duties of a sailing instructor. By doing so it also lends its own name and reputation to the instructor's credentials. US Sailing does this to provide uniform national standards on which everyone may rely. Aside from the instructor, those who benefit include the sailing public, employers, employment brokers, sailing schools, charter and rental agencies, insurance carriers, and any others who may find standardized skill documentation helpful in their decision making.

When an instructor lives up to the certification standards of US Sailing, it reinforces the value and perception of that certification for all who rely on it. If for any reason a certified instructor fails to live up to US Sailing standards, it reflects poorly on, and diminishes the value of, the credential for all US Sailing certified instructors.

So, once you become certified you represent US Sailing and reflect its standards every time you teach sailing. Among your primary professional responsibilities is a duty to US Sailing and your fellow certified instructors to live up to the standards of your certification credential.

Behavior & Appearance Guidelines for Instructors

Consumption of Alcohol: The use of alcohol and/or controlled substances during any course of training shall be considered as cause for suspension and/or dismissal.

Smoking: Smoking should be permitted only in appropriate areas outside the building, at breaks, and not be done below decks on any training vessel, power or sail.

Appearance: An instructor's appearance is directly related to your image as a professional. If you want to be taken seriously, look the part.

Clothing: Clean and neat, with no holes, tears or stains. No printing or illustration referring to alcohol, controlled substances, profanity or unprofessional behavior. Collared shirts are recommended. "Speedo" or bikini-type swimwear, bare chests, provocative attire and tank tops are discouraged in order to demonstrate proper role modeling. Instructor appearance should not be a distraction.

Hair: Neatly groomed, clean, tidy.

Footwear: Around waterfront and aboard boats, no bare feet or "flip-flops" at any time. Shoes should have closed toes and sides and have positive closure (laces or Velcro).

Caps and sunglasses: Caps, hats, or visors and sunglasses should not be worn indoors.

Life Jackets: Life jackets with holes or tears are illegal, and may not be used. Life jackets should be of the proper size, so they fit snugly. When afloat, life jackets should be zipped up.

Language: In order to create a more comfortable environment for learning, Instructors and ITs are not to engage in the use of profanity or any language or verbiage that would be reasonably construed a sexist, racist, off-color, vulgar, or otherwise inappropriate to their status as a professional sailing instructor. They shall also not condone such language in their students or in their courses.

Harassment and Abuse Awareness: ITs and Instructors need to be sensitive to perceived conduct and the effect it has on what is considered appropriate or inappropriate behavior. For instance, while it is generally considered that touches above the shoulder (a pat on the shoulder, a "high-five," a handshake, etc.) are acceptable, caution must exercised when other body contact is involved, including even a consoling hug. Teachers and counselors are told to avoid being in situations where they are alone with a student. While this may be a sad commentary on our times, it is important to be aware of these issues, and judgments.

Medications: Instructors should not give any prescription or non-prescription medications to adults or minors. Instructors may encourage adults and minors to follow the directions of prescriptions they may have. When dealing with minors and medications, they should obtain written consent from the parents/guardians of the minors. The medications must be in their own labeled medication containers with written instructions.

Behavior: Instructors, in any setting or gathering where they are perceived by others as representing US Sailing or their sailing employer, should recognize their responsibility as role models for their profession and conduct themselves as such in a professional responsible manner.

4. Responsibility to Yourself

To casual observers, teaching sailing appears to be a relaxing and easy-going occupation; but veteran instructors know that it can be quite challenging, both physically and mentally. To be fair to yourself and all those who rely on you, you need to stay healthy, alert, positive, and focused.

Personal Maintenance

There are innumerable stresses and pressures which can affect an instructor's health, moods, attitude, and job performance. To be at your resilient best day after day you need to be in the habit of performing routine preventive maintenance on yourself, just as you would on the boats on which you teach. Personal maintenance is an essential discipline for any serious professional.

By adhering to the following personal maintenance guidelines, you will be off to a good start:

- Get plenty of sleep.
- Eat regular, balanced meals.
- Maintain a low-fat diet.
- Exercise regularly.
- Drink plenty of water.
- Avoid caffeine.
- Don't smoke.
- Minimize alcohol consumption.
- Use sun protection (sunscreen, sunglasses, hat, etc.).
- Take regular days off, as needed.
- Make time for outside interests.

Stress Management

Stress gradually takes its toll when an instructor feels overwhelmed by job pressures. Frequent pressing deadlines, long hours, conflicts, high expectations, insufficient resources, emergencies, sudden setbacks, financial constraints, and preoccupying personal problems are only a few of the things instructors may face every day which contribute to stress.

Stress management is particularly important during a program's busy times. When tension and job pressures run high, the human body sometimes responds much as if it were in physical danger. It releases stress hormones into the bloodstream to prepare for self-preservation. This is a survival response which kicks the body into overdrive when there is threat of physical danger, but it is an overreaction for typical job stress. If it continues too long, it can gradually wear a person down and lead to physical and mental burnout. When there is too much to do, prioritize and delegate.

Occupational stress usually begins in the mind. When people "believe" they are under job pressure, their body follows their mind's lead. It tenses up. Some common symptoms of stress are fatigue, irritability, nervousness, headaches, sleep and eating disorders, difficulty concentrating, etc. Left unchecked, constant stress can weaken the body's immune system, increasing its vulnerability to a host of more serious illnesses.

Relaxation and exercise breaks are the most commonly prescribed everyday remedies for coping with stress. Though they both require an investment of time (something you -may think you have too little of already), many people find it a worthwhile trade, because afterward they are more productive and less anxious.

Occasional relaxation breaks can help relieve tension, restore equilibrium and keep your body and mind cooperating. Regular exercise is another popular and healthful way to relieve tension. As little as 20 minutes per day of aerobic activity (e.g., jogging, bicycling, tennis, etc.) can make a big difference in controlling stress.

Time Management

All busy productive people need to be time-conscious. If you linger too long on one task, you may not get another done. As job pressures pile up, and time runs short, you may find yourself choosing painfully between things to get done and things to neglect. Good time management can help get all the important things done on time.

First, carefully plan your day in advance. Write a "to do" list of everything you have to accomplish and prioritize it. That is, put the most important things first. Start early in the day, and do things in order of priority. That way, if you get derailed during the day by unexpected events, you will have completed the most important things.

Second, you can delegate tasks to others. Do not forget that parents are a resource that can alleviate your workload. Not everything needs to be done by you personally, and not everything needs to be absolutely perfect. If it does, delegate more judiciously.

Third, budget your time as though it were money. Do not allow open-ended parcels of time any more than you would write blank checks. Stick to your schedule. Tell others how much time you have available to spend with them. It will help to keep them focused and considerate of your schedule.

Fourth, when working with other instructors or staff members as a team, stick to a routine schedule as much as possible. Consider posting everyone's daily schedule (including temporary changes) on a bulletin board. Good teammates need to communicate frequently.

Knowing when and where to find one another saves everyone search and worry time, while minimizing the pitfalls of indirect or non-existent communication.

With good time management you can cover the distance even when job pressures build.

INSTRUCTORS TAKE NOTE...

Time management tips:

• Make a "to do" list every day.

• List most important things first.

• Start early in the day.

• Do things in order of priority.

• Delegate whenever possible.

• Budget time as though it were money.

• Tell people how much time you have for them.

• Stick to your schedule.

• Adhere to a daily routine.

Professional Training

Try to learn as much as you can about being a sailing instructor. US Sailing publishes many instructor manuals and student books. They also offer training courses like:

- Small Boat Sailing Level 1 Instructor,
- Small Boat Level 2 Coach or Senior Instructor,
- Advanced Coaching Level 3 Coach,
- Safe Powerboat Handling, and Safety, Rescue, and Support,
- Level 1 Windsurfing,
- Basic Keelboat Instructor, Cruising Instructor, Coastal Navigation Instructor, or Passagemaking Instructor.

It can also be helpful to attend such events as the National Sailing Programs Symposium or Advanced Coaching Symposium. Another way is to take some of the American Red Cross courses like Sport Safety Training, Community First Aid and Safety, Standard First Aid, Lifeguarding, and/or Basic Water Rescue.

Make sure you have any local, state or federal licenses that are necessary. Many sailing programs are concerned about U.S. Coast Guard (USCG) licensing for instructors who will be operating safety boats. Depending on how your program is run and what your safety boats are doing, you may or may not need a USCG license. Things can always change, but the following guidelines are the current situation.

USCG licenses are not required if:

- Your instructors are teaching on a non-motorized sailboat.
- Your instructors are teaching on a motorized safety boat without students on board.

USCG licenses are required if:

- Your safety boat is used to transport students, thus placing the boat in the category of "transporting passengers for hire."
- Your instructors are teaching on a motorized sailboat, for example, a Sonar with an outboard.
- Exceptions: A safety boat can be used for:
- Taking one or more students on board if they are injured, ill, fatigued, or frightened, and thus unable to sail their boats.
- Taking a boat under tow which has become disabled or which is in, or headed toward, a danger area.
- Assisting in capsize recovery or other emergency or rescue activity.
- Taking one or more boats under tow if weather conditions are deemed unsafe. Utilizing the boat as a static floating platform to assist in safely transferring a student from one boat to another.

US Sailing certification can help in getting a USCG license. The USCG considers US Sailing's Small Boat Sailing Level 1 Instructor, Basic Keelboat Instructor and Basic Keelboat Student certifications to be the equivalent of having taken a "safe boating course" -- one of the requirements for a USCG license. You can contact your nearest USCG office about obtaining a license.

Risk Management

Benefits and Risks of Teaching Sailing

It is not hard to appreciate all the benefits of employment as a sailing instructor. As part of your job you have an opportunity to work:

- outdoors and on the water,
- with co-workers around your age,
- independently,
- on your own coach's powerboat,
- teaching an age group you enjoy,
- in and around sailboats,
- with a class that recognizes you as an expert,
- and get paid.

There is no doubt that teaching sailing is a great job for anyone who loves sailing. In fact, who wouldn't want a job just like ours!

But it is easy to get caught up in the fun aspects of the job and lose sight of the incredible responsibility you have for the safety of your students. Rarely does the general public think about the inherent risks of sailing, and in many ways this is a good for sailing programs. It is preferable and beneficial that the public views learning to sail as a safe activity. If they didn't we would struggle to find students who would sign-up for sailing instruction. It also isn't the job of your students or their parents to constantly identify, assess, and avoid the risks of sailing. It is your job as a sailing instructor! Consider some of the risks in sailing.

- As an instructor, paid or volunteer, you have a legal and moral responsibility (**duty of care**) to your students, both kids and adults.
- Often we work with kids, a student group that requires increased supervision.
- The skill level of our students is often a beginner level, making the more dependent on their instructor.
- Our students spend most of their time in small boats in deep water.
- Teaching is usually done from a powerboat, a motor vehicle, which has its own set of risks and dangers.
- We do not control the environment where we work, from wind and waves, to heat or cold, to lightning, and even marine wildlife. We often have to respond to the environment rather than control the elements.

While it is typical that sailing instructors think about all of the great parts of their job, they often overlook the extent of their **liability**, the duties and risks for which an instructor is responsible. If an instructor does not demonstrate adequate **duty of care** to their students, property, and the environment, that instructor can be found guilty for the injury or death of a student, or the destruction of property. While the long-term psychological anguish for being negligent might be punishment enough, an instructor found negligent in court is subject to devastating monetary penalties and/or incarceration.

The following section reviews the intricacies of risk management, the methods and processes for recognizing risk, avoiding hazards and dealing with accidents when they occur.

Legal liability risks include two main areas.

- **Regulatory risks**

    These are responsibilities mandated by federal, state and local laws and regulations such as:

    - requiring launch operators to obtain appropriate licenses,
    - stipulating ways to control pollution,
    - seeking to protect wildlife such as manatees,
    - or requiring powerboats to be registered and inspected.

    These regulations include exposures such as those of employers to employees under state workers' compensation acts, the Jones Act and the Longshoremens' and Harborworkers' Act. Regulatory risks have remedies for wrongs such as fines, jail, or both and the violations may be either civil or criminal in nature.

- **Contracts and Tort Liability**

    Contractual liabilities can arise when a party to a written or verbal contract (such as a contract to provide sailing instruction) is held to have violated a responsibility under the terms of the contract. For both parties it is strongly advisable to have written contracts; verbal contracts can be actual or implied, and injuries can be real or imagined.

    Tort (injury) liability theories include **negligence,** assault, battery, defamation, invasion of privacy and the like. Most often the tort theory in sailing cases is negligence. Sailing instructors have a **duty of care** for their students. This is essentially doing or not doing something a reasonably careful person would or would not do. The liabilities are different when you are working with minors.

The following four **elements of negligence** must all be present for the court to determine negligence.

1. You must have a legal **duty to the injured party**.
2. You must have **failed to fulfill your duty.**
3. The **injury had to occur to the party** to whom you owed the duty.
4. Your **failure to fulfill your duty** has to be the **cause of the injury.**

There are three common **defenses for negligence** available to an instructor.

1. Show that the all the **elements of negligence were not present**.
2. Show that the direct causes of the injury were an **act of God** *(forces of nature)*.
3. Show that the injured party is guilty of ***contributory negligence,*** meaning that he or she caused the injury. ***Comparative negligence*** is when a proportion of the fault is distributed among several parties.

For example, imagine this fictitious but possible scenario. A class of kids is out sailing in their boats on a very light wind day. The boats are ghosting along, barely able to move. It is hot in the sun that day, and the instructor decides it would be fun to "wake" the sailors in their boats, splashing them and cooling them off from the heat with the wake from the safety boat. The instructor accelerates the powerboat to full throttle, driving right at a sailboat. At the last moment, they turn the wheel to avoid a collision, trying to sending a wave from the powerboat splashing over the sailors. But something goes wrong. The powerboat hits a wave oddly, or the steering cable sticks or breaks.

> **Instructors take note…**
>
> Be aware that just because a parent or student (if over 18 years old) signs a standard release form that actually doesn't absolve the instructor in any way from being negligent.

Perhaps the instructor's reaction time is off just a little. No matter the reason, the powerboat fails to turn in time and drives into the sailboat and sailors causing significant injury and damage.

The instructor in this situation may not have started out with a malicious thought or evil intent. They might have watched similar behavior from their own instructors years ago. However, what may have started out as a silly game, or relief from the boredom, or an effort to provide comfort from the heat has resulted in injury and damage. Depending on the severity of injuries and damage, or the will of the plaintiffs, this instructor, their co-workers, supervisor(s), club, any certifying agencies like US Sailing, the boat and engine manufacturers, etc. could end up in civil or criminal proceedings.

None of us believe something like the powerboat accident described above could happen to us…until it does happen to us. The reality is that accidents happen. Anywhere, anytime, anyplace an accident can happen. There may be no better summary than legal scholar Henry de Bracton's, "An ounce of prevention is worth a pound of cure." Failing to identify, prevent, notify and resolve risks could all result in negligence.

Legal Action

While there are a lot of jokes about lawyers and our litigious society, no party to a lawsuit sees their situation as a joke. The situation for a **civil lawsuit** usually involves an aggrieved party, the plaintiff, seeking monetary judgment for a harm or injury they have suffered. The plaintiff sues a defendant(s) who is defending their decisions and actions as meeting their duty of care. A **criminal case** is similar, except that instead of a monetary judgment, a conviction results in some type of incarceration for a criminal act. Either or both types of lawsuits could be brought against a sailing instructor for negligence. After hearing arguments from the plaintiff and defendant, a jury or judge will apply the law to determine guilt, innocence, or culpability-the shared percentage of responsibility.

Risk Management Goals

Almost all human activity involves the **risk** of injury. Teaching sailing is no exception. In turn, the **risk** a sailing instructor assumes involves the possibility of someone getting injured or damaging property and filing a lawsuit. To the most reasonable extent possible risks need to be managed, i.e. prevented or minimized, at all levels.

The primary goals of risk management are:

1. Through action, intervention, and notification **prevent injury or harm** to anyone, but students in particular.
2. to **recognize situations** that could result in harm to person or property and properly deal with them before an accident occurs,
3. to try to reduce the number of all accidents, even the ones that cause little harm but happen frequently,
4. to **be prepared for the contingency of an emergency** should harm actually occur, so that the harm is kept to a minimum, and,
5. to **monitor and adjust** as exposures change and develop.

Risk Management

In risk management we use a process for dealing with the risk which requires us to:

1. **Identify** risks,
2. **evaluate** the identified risks for the best treatment,
3. and **resolve** the identified risks.

Risk Identification

First perform a **site assessment.** This involves identifying those areas or items that may lead to an injury. This would mean checking and listing all items and areas around the facility, the docks and the boats themselves. On your list, include even the trivial. The more comprehensive the list the better prepared you will be. Something as simple as a splinter (from a dock covered in creosote) can lead to serious infection and possible gangrene if left unchecked. Site assessments are an ongoing process. The site and the situation change constantly in a marine environment and it is your job to be aware of these changes.

Risk Evaluation

Once your comprehensive list is made you can then organize it into one or two categories. One is comprised of areas or items that could lead to frequent and minor injuries, the other could lead to rare and serious injuries. Your goal will be to eliminate or reduce both the seriousness and the frequency of a potential injury.

Risk Resolution

There are four risk management techniques for risk resolution.

1. **Eliminate the risk.** An example would be to correct a problem by fixing a broken dock or not engaging in a particular activity.
2. **Reduce** the probability that the exposure will lead to serious injury. An example would be to require sailors to wear shoes.
3. **Assume the risk.** Since students have to go out on the water to sail, an example would be to accept the risk and manage the exposure.
4. **Transfer the risk to a third party.** An example would be to buy lunch from a vendor instead of making lunch for the class or to obtain insurance and have an insurance company take the risk.

Risk Control

Starting with the top priority risks, program organizers should develop a series of responses to try to prevent an occurrence and to be prepared should a contingency occur. They should have a written Emergency Action Plan, and they should have all instructors participate in actual "practice drills." If some portions of a program are deemed too hazardous, they should be properly removed. For example, an overhead electrical wire anywhere near a small boat launching area is clearly unacceptable. It should be removed or run underground. Other risks can be managed by safety instruction. For example, wearing **life jackets** at all times on the water may not prevent a drowning but will surely reduce significantly the possibility of one. Still others will require well thought-out emergency planning, such as responses for squalls and similar sudden weather changes.

Risk Financing

Funds must be budgeted for a wide variety of risk controls and, in addition, for the more remote possibility that additional costs may be incurred because of loss or damage to property, injury to others, including damage to their property, and regulatory fines. Any program will be wise to have a defined contingency reserve to draw against for smaller cost situations, plus prudent insurance to protect the sponsoring organization, its employees, and volunteers. *Instructors have a right to know exactly what financial protection has been arranged on their behalf by the sponsoring organization.*

Documentation and record keeping

The importance of proper record keeping cannot be over emphasized. Maintain a complete record of all forms, agreements, reports, checklists, etc. If an injury was to occur and a lawsuit is filed, complete documentation of your efforts will be essential for a successful defense. You must maintain records of all actions taken to avoid an accident and what actually happened. These records may be all you have to show a jury that the defendant(s) acted in a prudent and professional manner, and may very well be the difference in prevailing in a lawsuit.

Risk Management Conclusion

Risk management in sailing is essentially common sense. Cautious sailors respect the sea, its power and vagaries, and the fragility of their equipment. This essential caution will be taught by prudent sailing instructors to their students, using the tools of risk assessment, risk control, and risk financing, to assure a safe and secure program -- one that enhances the joy of the sport of sailing.

Even with all of these precautions taken, an accident can still happen. It may also end up in court with a judge awarding damages to the injured party, even though you feel you performed as well as anyone could have in the same situation. Our ultimate goal is for you, as an instructor, to be confident in knowing that you have done everything that could have been done in each situation to ensure a safe program for all.

Teaching Theory

This section connects the theory of learning, teaching, sports psychology, communication skills, and leadership to the practice of everyday sailing instruction. It is intended to help the new instructor to establish fundamental skills and develop an individual teaching style.

New instructors should bear in mind that no text or training program can fully prepare a sailing instructor for every eventuality. So *flexibility* is the sailing instructor's watchword. The importance of maintaining that flexibility is the underlying message summed up in the Instructor Trainers' familiar catch-phrase, *monitor and adjust*.

There are few absolutes in sailing instruction. It is at least as much art as science, so plenty of room remains for an instructor's personal creativity. An instructor frequently needs to be resourceful, creative, and prepared to modify and adapt any lesson plan to the circumstances of the moment.

Overall, it is good advice to remain faithful to the fundamentals without being afraid to build on them and experiment with a bit of your own creativity. Providing for safety, fun and learning are the only unalterable requirements in sailing instruction.

How People Learn

Everybody's Different

No two students of sailing are exactly the same. Each brings a unique combination of background information, skills, hopes, fears, motives, and native talent. To some, sailing seems to come naturally; to others it is mysterious and confusing. Some easily grasp concepts but falter with hands-on skills. Others are agile and dexterous but struggle with theory and concepts. The unique mixture of attributes each student possesses presents a unique challenge to an instructor.

INSTRUCTORS TAKE NOTE...

- Different people learn differently -- including instructors.
- Teaching methods which once helped you to learn may not be effective for all of your students.
- If a student does not learn, the teaching is ineffective.
- The instructor succeeds only when the student does.

Left to their own devices, new untrained instructors are often inclined to teach sailing the way they learned it themselves. They reason that "if it worked for me, it will work for you too." Unfortunately, the "good for me/good for you" method often achieves only limited success. It appeals to the instructor's personal learning style but not necessarily to that of every student. As a result, some students learn quickly; others do not. A novice instructor, who is not familiar with the differences in the way people learn, may unfairly blame the student.

The truth is, if a student does not learn, the teaching is ineffective. All willing students have the capacity to learn. It is the instructor's job to determine how to best reach each individual and get the job done. The instructor succeeds only when the student does.

Veteran instructors can attest that a teaching technique which works well for one student may not necessarily work at all for another. If all people learned the same way, teaching sailing would be a simple matter. But people are different.

Among their personal differences is the way people perceive, store, process, and recall information. The following section explores some key elements of how people learn and how different people learn differently

Sensory Input

Because learning is the goal of teaching, an instructor should be familiar with the learning process. Learning begins with sensory input. Sensory input is the "raw data" taken in through the five senses: seeing, hearing, smelling, tasting and feeling (touch/movement).

Information is taken in through the 5 senses.

The senses are stimulus gatherers which feed information to the brain for processing. In sailing instruction we primarily employ just three of those senses, **seeing, hearing, and feeling.**

A Selective Process

In processing, storing, and retrieving sensory information, everyone's brain operates a little differently. How we learn best and fastest varies from person to person. Some of us rely on, or favor, particular senses over others.

Specifically, some people remember best what they see. They are *visual learners*. Others remember best what they hear. They are *auditory learners*. Still others remember best what they physically feel and do. They are *kinesthetic learners*. Some people learn equally well all three ways.

All of us are capable of learning through every one of our available senses. A person who favors or relies on one sense over another is neither unable to learn, nor necessarily learns poorly, through the non-dominant senses. All senses pitch in to some degree. The proportions simply vary from one individual to another.

Visual Learners

A visual learner imprints and retains information most effectively when it is presented visually, such as in pictures, graphics, videos, diagrams, demonstrations, etc.

Because of this affinity for visual input, a visual learner's memory is, in a sense, photographic. For example, a visual learner may recall not just a particular illustration from a textbook, but often its location on the page as well. A visual learner would also get more out of seeing a demonstration of tacking, rigging or docking than simply hearing them explained.

Visual learners retain better and faster when they can see what they are learning.

INSTRUCTORS TAKE NOTE...

When learning to sail, students use three of the five senses:

- Seeing
- Hearing
- *Feeling* (physical touch, movement)

Some students favor one sense over another -some may learn faster by seeing or doing something rather than by just hearing it explained.

Auditory Learners

An auditory learner learns most effectively when information is conveyed with sound. Because they remember best what they hear, auditory learners may easily recall conversations word-for-word. They may also recall details of each speaker's accent, tone of voice, and inflection. A person weak in auditory learning skills might only be able to remember the gist of the same conversation, while being less certain about precise phrasing and topic sequencing.

Kinesthetic Learners

A kinesthetic learner learns best by doing. Touching, physical manipulation, and the physical sensation of movement are what imprint information most easily in the kinesthetic learner's memory. A kinesthetic learner often becomes restless and bored during plain speeches and lectures, because simple listening is too passive. A

> Kinesthetic learners retain better and faster when they can <u>touch, feel or manipulate</u> what they are learning about.

kinesthetic learner retains information better when it is incorporated into some sort of physical activity. Reading material is best conveyed to the kinesthetic by linking it to a physical activity such as underlining, highlighting, copying it over, or reciting it aloud. A favorite kinesthetic/auditory teaching technique of grade school teachers is to set repetitive rote learning to music or poetry and have the class sing or recite it together. Singing the alphabet is one familiar example.

Get Your Three Senses In

Researchers estimate that roughly 70% of the general population is visual learners, about 25% are auditory learner, and approximately 5% are kinesthetic learners. Kids tend to be more kinesthetic than adults. As an instructor, you may find that sailors tend to be more kinesthetic than the general population.

When teaching a new sailing class, an instructor may presume there is a mix of each type of learner present. Though the instructor may not know who's who, it does not particularly matter, provided the instructor employs techniques which reach all three learning modes. If so, every student can learn. None is excluded or left behind.

All senses help in learning, but, for many people, some senses help more than others.

Visual Teaching Techniques include the use of:

- Gestures
- Graphs
- Facial expressions
- Color-coding
- Body language
- Text illustrations

- Hand signals
- Handouts
- Chalkboard illustrations
- Props
- Physical demonstrations
- Videos

There are lots of ways to make your teaching more visual.

Auditory Teaching Techniques include the use of

- Speech
- Whistle signals

- Loud hailers
- Audio equipment
- Instructor's voice: volume, tone, expressiveness, animation, and word choice

Auditory techniques are **most helpful on the water** where distance from students is greater.

Kinesthetic Teaching Techniques include the use of

- Hands-on participation
- Rote recitation
- Land drills
- Copying/note taking

- Water drills
- Take-home projects
- Reading aloud
- Simulator practice

There are plenty of techniques to turn a boring lecture into a fun activity or game.

The simple self-test that follows will help you understand more about your own sensory preference. Try it.

Self-Test #1: Sensory Preference

The following self-test is designed to help you understand whether you learn best by seeing, hearing or doing. By becoming more aware of your own learning style you will be better equipped to understand the differences in your students and adjust your teaching techniques to their needs.

This is not a timed test. You will not be graded. Simply answer each question honestly and total up your score at the end. Do not dwell on any particular question. Your first impulse usually provides the best response.

Directions: Score each of the statements below using the following point scale.

OFFEN = 5   SOMETIMES = 3   SELDOM = 1

1. _____ I remember more about a subject by listening than reading about it.
2. _____ I am better at following written directions than oral ones.
3. _____ When learning something new I like to jot down notes to review later.
4. _____ I bear down hard when I write with a pen or pencil.
5. _____ I require explanations of graphs, diagrams or visual directions.
6. _____ I like working with tools.
7. _____ I like and have little difficulty developing graphs and charts.
8. _____ I can easily tell if sounds match when I hear pairs of sounds.
9. _____ I remember things best when I write them down several times.
10. _____ I can understand and follow directions on maps.
11. _____ I learn school material better by listening to lectures and recordings.
12. _____ I play with coins, keys or other objects in my pockets.
13. _____ I can remember how to spell words better if I say the letters out loud rather than write them down.
14. _____ I understand news items better when I read them in the paper rather than listening to the radio.
15. _____ I chew gum or snack while I study.
16. _____ I find that the best way to remember something is to visualize it in my mind.
17. _____ I learn to spell words by writing imaginary letters with my finger tips.
18. _____ I prefer to listen to a good lecture or speech than read a text on the same subject.
19. _____ I am good at working and solving jigsaw puzzles and mazes.
20. _____ I grip or fiddle with objects while I am learning something new.
21. _____ I'd rather listen to the news on a radio than read about it in a newspaper.
22. _____ I get information on interesting subjects by reading about them.
23. _____ I am uncomfortable hugging, handshaking, touching others, etc.
24. _____ I am better at following spoken directions than written ones.

Scoring: Copy the point value from each of the above questions onto the correspondingly numbered spaces below. Total each column to obtain your personal sensory preference values.

VISUAL		AUDITORY		KINESTHETIC	
No.	Pts.	No.	Pts.	No.	Pts.
2	_____	1	_____	4	_____
3	_____	5	_____	6	_____
7	_____	8	_____	9	_____
10	_____	11	_____	12	_____
14	_____	13	_____	15	_____
16	_____	18	_____	17	_____
20	_____	21	_____	19	_____
22	_____	24	_____	23	_____
Total =_____		Total =_____		Total =_____	

Adapted from the original Barsch Learning Style Inventory by Dr. Jeffrey Barsch, EdD. with permission of Academic Therapy Publications, 20 Commercial Blvd., Novato, CA 94947

Multiple Pathways Teaching

As a rule, the more student sensory pathways an instructor can bring into play the better. A student's retention is generally higher and there is less confusion when multiple sensory pathways receive an integrated unambiguous message simultaneously.

Ideally, the student should see, hear, and do, all at once. Auditory teaching techniques, such as lecturing, may work adequately for highly auditory learners. Visual techniques, such as demonstrations, may work fine for highly visual learners. Yet, combining auditory with visual teaching techniques (e.g., explaining while demonstrating) works even better for both auditory *and* visual learners. Better still, blending visual, auditory *and* kinesthetic techniques (e.g., telling, showing and the students doing) improves learning for all students.

Multiple Pathways Teaching -using 2-3 senses instead of just 1.

The use of integrated visual, auditory, and kinesthetic teaching techniques allows every student to learn the way that suits him or her best, while receiving the same reinforcing message through their non-dominant senses. Learning takes place better and faster, and a class of students is more likely to progress at a uniform pace. As a bonus, multiple pathway teaching livens up the teaching environment, makes it more fun, and helps to raise motivation and morale.

Processing Information

The human brain is the most sophisticated information processor known, far out-pacing the ability of the most advanced computer. Science's understanding of how a brain works is evolving, but still subject to multiple theories.

> **INSTRUCTORS TAKE NOTE...**
>
> To reach all types of learners:
>
> - Show them (visual)
> - *Tell them* (auditory)
> - *Let* them do it (kinesthetic)

Applying the best theories about how brain functions in learning sailing is important in becoming an effective instructor, coach and teacher. Our job is not learning neural science, it is to determine what methods are best for teaching sailing to a variety of information processing preferences.

Concrete and Abstract Instruction

Every student's brain processes information differently. We already know that we have to use different teaching methods to reach all of our students by using kinesthetic, visual and auditory methods of instruction. Some students will prefer concrete information and answers, others may connect more with abstract instruction. Here is an example of the same concept in both a concrete and abstract form:

Concrete: Push the tiller toward the sail to head up.

Abstract: Heading up is caused the rudder deflecting water, creating a difference in pressure along the rudder blade.

Both statements are true. Knowing each individual student will help an instructor determine which method will be most helpful.

Teaching sailing presents many possibilities for using both concrete and abstract methods. To some degree the age and experience of students may determine how much an Instructor should lean towards concrete or abstract instruction. Consider the following example on teaching students how to make a boat move.

A concrete method is an effective way to teach, but might be most useful for younger students in the pre-teens to early teens age group or a real beginning student. The concrete lesson would focus more on teaching students to pull in the mainsheet until the sail stops luffing or easing the sheet until the sail is on the verge of a luff to make the boat move. For concrete instruction, an emphasis should be put on auditory and kinesthetic teaching methods.

Now let's look at how to teach making a boat move using abstract methods. While the concrete instruction is accurate, many students will struggle to comprehend this topic without knowing the details or abstract elements of how a boat moves. It is convenient and practical to think that abstract lessons are often better for students that already understand and properly perform a skill, but crave deeper understanding.

The abstract lesson on how a boat moves would focus on wind flow, high and low pressure, lift from sails and underwater fins. They are all concepts, or must be conceptualized by the student in order to learn the material. Excellent visuals, diagrams and drawings are usually emphasized to help learners connect with the information.

Usually when teaching concrete lessons, it is helpful to provide students with absolutes that indicate how to determine when to start or stop an action. For making a boat move, the absolute is adjusting the sail to the verge of a luff. It is a constant that never changes unless the boat is sailed in push mode and luffing is no longer possible, but then other constants can be taught. Here are some other useful examples of constants:

1) When to straighten the helm when tacking?
   (a) Many instructors would teach students to stop turning when they were on the new close hauled course. But how does a beginning student know that?
   The constant is when the sails fill on the new tack, that is the time to straighten the helm.

2) Which way does the tiller go in a tack? Jibe?
   (a) Many Instructors would teach students to move the tiller towards or away from the sailor. But who knows if a beginning sailor will sit in the correct spot.
   The constant for the tiller should reference the boom. The boom is always in the same spot to leeward and creates a better constant when teaching which way the tiller goes.

When teaching abstract elements of sailing, using analogies for learning bridges will make the information more accessible. For example, when talking about apparent wind, referring to the wind that is felt while riding a bicycle or sticking a hand out the window will help students learn concepts and theories through things they already know.

The Processing Loop

An effective Instructor will always help a student learn faster than if the student attempted to self-teach. While this is intuitive, the reason why Instructors accelerate the learning process may not be so clear.

However, understanding the processing loop should reinforce not only why an instructor improves learning, but how to apply lessons from Teaching Fundamentals to be most effective.

The Self-Taught Student

Step 1: Input

In a self-taught model a student gains information through input. The input may be appropriate, but the student cannot know whether they have the right input or not.

Step 2: Practice

After taking in the input, a student practices a skill. The practice may be correct, but the primary measure is if they have survived the experience.

Step 3: Self Assessment

The practice concludes and the student undertakes some self-assessment to reflect on and improve the original input, creating a new understanding to initiate more practice. The self-taught sailor cannot be certain that the self-assessment is accurate, but will find out in the process of more practice.

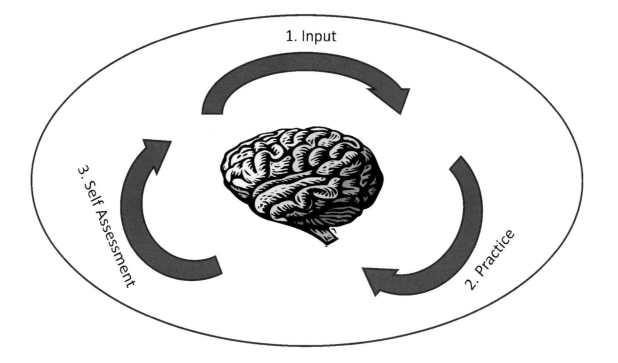

Instructed Student

Feedback

One of the most notable improvements gained from instruction is Feedback. Feedback includes positive reinforcement, skill correction, comprehension checks, rewards and encouragement. Feedback from the instructor comes in between the three brain processes, and occur multiple times during one lesson. From the student's perspective, feedback allows the following:

- the opportunity to ask questions,
- the potential for a comprehension check and feedback from the Instructor,
- the possibility of learning errors being corrected during the learning phase (see page ???)
- encouragement and rewards in the form of positive reinforcement, intrinsic and extrinsic rewards

Step 1: Learned Input

The instructed student gains an advantage immediately because they start with learned input, the correct information at an appropriate level. The input is delivered using the right balance of methods (visual, auditory and kinesthetic) and using an abstract or concrete framework that reduces confusion of interpretation.

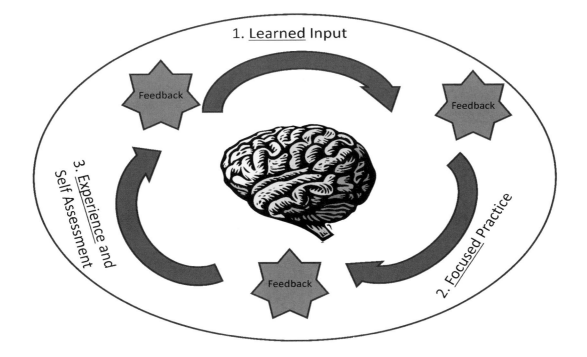

Step 2: Focused Practice

Once the student learns something new and gains the insight provided by input, they are ready to start practicing the new skill. An Instructor can focus a drill on the specific skill being learned, allowing a student to really develop the critical information and physical executions necessary to perform the skill properly. Through feedback during the practice, the skill is continually improved during the consolidation phase.

Step 3: Experienced Assessment

As the student finishes practice and receives experienced assessment through review and comprehension checks, they advance their initial understanding at Step 1, input. Continuing this loop finally allows a student to move toward automation phase, when the skill can be performed without conscious thought. An example of automation is riding a bike. When first learning how to ride, a student thinks about balance, peddling, steering, etc. As the skill develops the ability reaches a point where it is unnecessary to think about balance, peddling and steering, they just happen.

The following sections elaborate on the various components of the processing loop.

What Am I??? New instructors ought to spend some time becoming familiar with their own learning and problem solving characteristics. An instructor's personal learning style favoritism or bias could blind him to the learning needs of students who require a different approach.

The previous self-test should help you to understand a bit more about your own learning style. After taking self-test 1ask yourself:

- Do I favor one sensory pathway over another?
- Do I respond better to one teaching technique than another?
- How much does it influence the way I teach and communicate with others.
- Do I recognize and understand those differences in others?
- Am I patient with those who learn differently?
- What modifications could I make in my teaching style to accommodate them?

> **INSTRUCTORS TAKE NOTE...**
>
> Understanding your own learning style is the best starting point before teaching others. It includes understanding how you yourself perceive, process and store information.
>
> The Sensory Preference Self-Test will help you understand your own strengths and weaknesses in how you perceive the world around you.

<u>**Know your Students**</u>

Equally important to knowing your learning preference is knowing your student's learning preferences. It is the critical element to providing a productive learning environment. You should be prepared to adjust your teaching style to reach all your students, not just a few. To do that well it is helpful to know yourself, understand your students, carefully monitor student responsiveness, and adjust your teaching style to meet them on their own mental turf. The different student groups to consider include student's age, gender, physical or mental capabilities, and cultural background. Just as people have different learning preferences, they will also have different comfort levels and preferences in a learning environment. If you have difficulty meeting the expectations of your students, speak to them individually or as a group to learn more effective ways of helping them feel comfortable.

Multiple Pathways Teaching

Untrained or careless instructors sometimes refer to classroom teaching sessions as *lectures*. The word *lecture* carries a negative connotation and should be avoided. Lectures and speeches are very boring to many students, particularly to the visual and kinesthetic learners. Unless the instructor is a truly gifted or charismatic speaker, plain lecturing is a poor teaching technique. It appeals mainly to the auditory learners present, only 25% of a typical group. A trained instructor uses many communication techniques in classroom teaching besides simple speech.

> **INSTRUCTORS TAKE NOTE...**
>
> *Chalk talks* should be kept to 10 minutes because of a student's attention span and comprehension ability for new material.

Some instructors prefer to call classroom teaching *chalk talks*, because they illustrate the lesson on a chalkboard while they speak. Students retain more from chalk talks than from plain lectures because of the visual assistance of the chalkboard. Visual aids, of course, appeal to the visual learners; and both auditory and visual learners learn better when they see and hear the same message together. Chalk talks appeal to a much broader audience than plain lectures, roughly 95% compared to 25%.

Better still, combining auditory, visual, and kinesthetic teaching techniques usually achieves the best results of all. Neither auditory nor visual techniques appeal to the kinesthetic learner as much as *doing*. Kinesthetic learners often fidget and lose concentration in a sedentary or passive learning environment. Veteran instructors know that active physical involvement coordinated with auditory and visual support works best for virtually every type of learner.

An instructor who simply stands still and lectures on how to furl a sail will get very poor learning results. An instructor who uses an actual sail while explaining furling will have far greater success. But the instructor who takes it a step further, getting the students physically involved, hands-on, manipulating a real sail will achieve the best results of all. Seeing, hearing and doing --these three methods combined teach the best

Illustrate Your Point

Get in the habit of drawing diagrams, writing outlines, or somehow illustrating your key points on a chalkboard, where they can visually reinforce your lesson and silently repeat it as often as your students glance at the board. Strategically pausing now and then to draw on a

> - Illustrate your point whenever possible.
> - Diagrams and hands-on demonstrations are what hold the attention of the visual and kinesthetic learners.

chalkboard also provides students with some helpful assimilation time and you with a moment to collect your thoughts.

When giving chalk talks avoid talking into the board. Pause to write or draw as needed; but then stand aside and turn to face your students when you speak. Block no one's view, and be sure everyone can hear you clearly. Be conscious of the visual cut-off angle your body creates. When giving chalk talks, demonstrations or any presentation, arrange student seating in a semi-circle or horseshoe large enough for everyone to see clearly. *Stand* aside so everyone can see.

Utilizing Resources

There are many books, magazines, videos and teaching aids which can be used to augment your teaching. Some, like the *Small Boat Sailor Certification Record Book* (known as the "Little Red Book"), and the *Learn Sailing Right!* book are available from US Sailing along with many other products. Don't forget your local libraries, museums, marine stores, book stores, sailing lofts, boat builders, sailing related industries and "hot shot" sailors --all are excellent resources.

<u>Interactive Teaching</u>

Not every topic, however, lends itself easily to hands-on kinesthetic teaching techniques. Some topics involve concepts, rather than physical skills, and are the most challenging when teaching kinesthetic learners. Interactive teaching is quite often an effective method. The following are among the most common interactive teaching techniques in sailing instruction.

> **INSTRUCTORS TAKE NOTE...**
>
> Passive "sit and listen" lectures are not very effective for most types of learners. Chalk talks get much better results, because they include a visual component. Better still are interactive (kinesthetic) teaching techniques which also involve active student participation.

The Discovery Method is also known as the *Socratic Method.* It involves posing a series of easily answered questions which guide the class to a conclusion foreseen by the instructor. In response to the instructor's "loaded" questions, students volunteer answers. Each answer is a step toward a broader conclusion. This method works particularly well if the pace is quick and lively, the instructor illustrates each point on the chalkboard and the instructor actively involves and draws out responses from every student. It is a common mistake to think that the desired series of question are easily made off the cuff. Planning the questions is integral to a lesson just like planning the chalk talk or water drill. Be sure to think through your questions to make sure that your audience will understand the questions and be able to provide the desired answers.

Example:

Question 1:	"What stops a sailboat from side-slipping?"
Answer 1:	"Centerboard, daggerboard or keel"
Question 2:	"On which point of sail is it needed least?"
Answer 2:	"Running"
Question 3:	"How can you reduce underwater resistance on a centerboard boat when running?"
Answer 3:	"Raise the centerboard"

Discovery Questions help a student assimilate information by pressing the student to focus on the topic, think independently and actively respond. It also provides the instructor with valuable feedback on each student's level of understanding. However, teaching by guided discovery does not always draw out the desired responses right away. Sometimes the question must be repeated or rephrased. Reaching a desired conclusion sometimes can be unpredictably time consuming, so it may not always be a practical teaching technique when class time runs short.

When it is necessary to keep the class moving along, a discovery/chalk-talk combination can help speed up the lesson. To save time, the instructor can shift to the speedier, self-pacing chalk-talk method of presenting the material, pausing only as time allows by engaging students with leading questions. By limiting interaction this way, the instructor gains more control over the pace. The trade-off is the risk of sacrificing some effectiveness. Maintaining as much active student participation as time and circumstances allow is the key to overall effectiveness in classroom teaching techniques.

The Listing Technique is another variation on the Discovery Method. It is most suitable for teaching topics with a series of related elements.

> **Example:** "What items do you think ought to be included on a pre-sail checklist."

Each student is invited to provide an answer. The instructor lists the responses on the chalkboard. As the list grows, it serves as a constant visual reinforcement, imprinting the information in the students' visual memory. The technique helps maintain the class' attention, because the students are active contributors to a visible product.

The Pros and Cons Technique is a further variation on the Listing Technique. It is useful for topics where the intent is to emphasize or clarify advantages, disadvantages, differences and limitations.

> **Example:** "Compared to planing hull vessels, can you think of any performance advantages or disadvantages of displacement hulls?"

The instructor makes two side-by-side lists of student responses on the board, one for advantages, one for disadvantages. The two lists visually reinforce the students' auditory input. The side-by-side display encourages visual comparison, and the interaction

Challenge Questions ask a specific question of a particular student without seeking other volunteers.

Example: "Susie, Which way should you move the tiller to jibe?"

In a shy, passive or reluctant group it presses every student to engage the topic and actively participate in the discussion. The

Instructors Take Caution!
Calling on unaware students has the potential for embarrassing those who may have been momentarily distracted.

class is likely to remain particularly alert, since no student knows who may be called on next for a response. Additionally, challenge questioning allows an instructor to assess if a particular student, who may have been struggling with the lesson, has learned the information.

However, the Challenge Technique has the potential to be misused as a way to "catch" someone who was not paying attention. Additionally, when one student is called upon for an answer, all the other students can tune out because they are relieved of having to answer.

Teaching Physical Skills

A student normally passes through three general phases in acquiring a new physical skill: *learning, consolidation,* and *automation.*

In the learning phase, a student receives new input or information on how to perform a new skill, such

☞ **INSTRUCTORS TAKE NOTE...**
Focus on teaching essential core skills until students are near to mastery before you address lower priority technical improvements.

as tacking. An instructor may introduce the skill as a concept or theory in a classroom setting at first. There it can be established how, when and why the skill is used. Analogies are helpful in the learning phase, so a student may relate new ideas to something familiar. Then the instructor divides or explains the new skill into digestible steps. Each step is described and demonstrated in its proper sequence before the students try it for themselves.

A slow motion walk-through or *land drill* is helpful at first, because they incorporate a kinesthetic element to the instruction and provide more assimilation time than a real-life tack. Whenever a skill is completely new to the student, it may be useful to slow the pace and provide step-by-step feedback and encouragement. As the student catches on, the pace of the skill can be accelerated gradually until they reach "real time," actual speed. Then the student is ready to practice and consolidate a "real" tack.

> ☞ **INSTRUCTORS TAKE NOTE...**
>
> *Land Drills* are important when introducing a new skill.

An instructor may spot several errors in the student's first efforts but should resist the temptation to blurt them all out at once. Keep it simple. Using the *feedback sandwich,* first find something to praise, then zero in on the correction. In general, focus on only one or two errors at a time, with the most important first. Always end with an encouraging word. Positive reinforcement is very important in sustaining motivation in the learning and consolidation phases. Be patient and enthusiastic.

The type of feedback an instructor should offer during the learning phase depends on whether mistakes are *learning* or *performance* errors.

> A ***learning error*** is a mistake due to misunderstanding the correct way to perform a skill. For example, a student who mistakenly pushes the tiller to leeward in order to jibe-even though the instructor told them to move the tiller away from the sail, may not have understood which way to move the tiller from the outset. If so, it is a learning error. In such a case the instructor needs to rephrase or re-teach the original instruction on how to perform the skill.
>
> A ***performance error*** is not a mistake of understanding, rather one of execution. For example, a student who over-steers in a jibe may understand the correct steps involved in jibing but needs only to refine their execution. Appropriate action, therefore, would be a *feedback sandwich* rather than a full repetition of the original lesson on how to jibe.

Whether correcting a performance or a learning error, an instructor should be alert and respond promptly. Corrective feedback should be immediate whenever possible, so a mistake does not get a chance to become a habit. An error undetected is an error uncorrected.

In the consolidation phase, a student practices merging the steps into a single smooth coordinated maneuver, and may need only occasional correction and encouragement.

> ☞ **INSTRUCTORS TAKE NOTE...**
>
> *Water Drills* are an important teaching tool in the consolidation phase.

In this second phase a student may become so absorbed in the challenge of performance that his or her awareness and concentration level reaches a peak. This is a critical period where the student is learning by doing, experimenting, and to some extent, self-correcting and even self-reinforcing.

In the consolidation phase, processing a skill occurs mostly kinesthetically and visually. While practicing the new skill, the student receives steady instant feedback simply by feeling and observing the consequences (tiller and sheet pressure, wind and hull velocity changes, heel changes, amount of luff, etc.) of his/her actions.

Feeling and observing the fluctuations of all the variables is a critical part of learning to sail. Repetition builds channels of kinesthetic memory so that complex skills are gradually performed more smoothly, with less awkwardness and hesitation.

Refrain from unnecessarily interrupting this valuable processing-by-doing stage with excessive feedback. Students should not be prevented from making all mistakes. Experiencing the consequences of performance errors is a vital and productive part of learning to sail. Unless there is physical danger or you see a performance or learning error, be patient. Simply observe from a non-distracting distance until your comments are truly needed.

In the automatic phase the student understands what is required and performs the maneuver consistently and competently. This is a confidence building period which then paves the way to the next skill in the lesson plan. In the automation phase skills are executed without conscious thought. In the same manner that someone may walk between classrooms in a school, make turns and avoid other people while thinking about something altogether different, a sailor has automated a skill when they no longer need to consciously think about the skill, they just do it.

The Feedback Sandwich

Providing constructive criticism will allow students to focus on areas that concern them exclusively and alert them to specific areas where they need to learn or practice for mastery. When teaching a new skill, an instructor's casual blunt criticism may sometimes discourage the very behavior it is intended to improve.

Critical remarks should be constructive and worded tactfully. When an instructor critiques a student's performance, negative feedback should be surrounded with encouragement. If, for example, Abby over-steers when tacking, and the instructor simply comments, "That was a lousy tack," Abby learns nothing useful and may very well feel hurt or discouraged by her instructor's terse and callous remark. Look to turn negative comments into positive ones. For example, instead of saying "you won't go faster if you sit in the wrong place" try saying "you will go faster if you sit in the right place." Students respond much better to positive, rather than negative comments.

In *a feedback sandwich* the instructor gets the message across without the sting of criticism by layering positive, constructive, and specific feedback, like a sandwich, in between slices of positive feedback. The instructor starts off with a positive remark, such as "Good effort, Abby. You nearly nailed it that time."

Then the instructor slips in the constructive part of the feedback, "but you over-steered a bit," tactfully sparing Abby's ego by focusing on the specific part of the maneuver which did not measure up.

Remember, feedback sandwiches are about **fault correction** and **reinforcement**.

Then the instructor constructively offers a remedy to the problem, "Begin to straightening your course a little sooner after the tack, and your tacks will be much smoother." And finally the instructor leaves the student with a positive and encouraging comment, "Let me see you try it again. I know you can do this."

A tactful *feedback sandwich* is perceived positively and can boost motivation. Instructors need to be aware of how their comments are perceived and felt, so they can avoid the pitfalls of negativity. Obvious and potentially embarrassing student mistakes, such as accidental collisions, do not need to be pointed out at all. Announcing the event across the water to the whole group may only add humiliation to an already embarrassing situation. It would be more constructive to use the experience as a teaching tool, helping the students understand what went wrong and how to prevent a recurrence.

Feedback Follow-up

Once an instructor has provided feedback, be prepared to follow-up on your recommendations. Watch how the student applies your feedback to make sure the corrections are being applied properly. If the student needs more feedback on the same skill, be prepared to rephrase the feedback, or review elements the student may be missing. If a student performs the corrections from your feedback, recognize the improvement before moving on to new feedback sandwiches will be a strong reinforcement. Remember, feedback is an ongoing process for each student.

Monitor and Adjust

Despite great planning and lesson organization, there will be surprises that arise. Perhaps students struggle with consolidating a skill, or the weather changes, or someone gets injured. There are unknown occurrences that will force an instructor to change their plan. The more an instructor can anticipate potential problems and make adjustments, the smoother, more effective a lesson will go.

Teaching vs. Coaching

When teaching a new skill an instructor must be patient, methodical, and very encouraging. High quality performance is not the object when learning a new skill. Simply imprinting the sequence of the individual component steps of a maneuver is the initial mission (the learning phase). Once the student can reliably perform the maneuver (the automatic phase), however awkwardly, coaching takes over from teaching.

Coaching is a training regimen geared toward improving existing skills more so than learning brand new ones. Teaching and coaching techniques are quite similar, but they are different in one important aspect. In coaching, the instructor generally employs an intermittent positive reinforcement schedule, rather than a regular one. That is, by selectively reinforcing a behavior, the instructor can gradually raise the stakes, shaping performance by praising only improved performance rather than mere adequacy. The student is encouraged to improve performance by the instructor's increasingly higher standards and expectations.

Communication

Productive teaching begins with clear communication. Communication is successful when an intended message is accurately conveyed by the instructor and understood by the student. But it is not a simple matter of, "I talk. You listen." The everyday communication between instructor and student has many elements. Some are obvious, others quite subtle. The following section explores the complexities of communicating effectively, both on and off the water.

Classroom Presentation Skills

Preparation for teaching should begin long before the class starts. In a format with no pre-designed curriculum or course outline, a detailed written plan should be prepared daily by the instructor. It should have:

- clearly stated goals,
- topic sequence,
- teaching method,

- equipment requirements,
- time allotments,
- and a method for evaluating results

Before class all teaching materials, handouts, audio and visual aids and props should be checked carefully. Once class begins, it should flow smoothly and without interruption. Awkward pauses to locate, organize, or repair teaching aids disrupts student concentration, diminish confidence, and make it difficult to maintain control of the teaching environment.

Repetition is a normal and necessary part of teaching. The more important a point is, the more important it is to repeat it. There are several good reasons to repeat information. Some students may not have been paying attention the first time. Some may have not heard you clearly. Some may have not understood fully. Repetition gives them another chance to learn and you another chance to succeed. There is an old saying, `three times for the average mind.'

Psychology of Learning

Behavioral Psychology offers a good deal of insight into individual learning behavior in sailing instruction. In experimental psychology, the training process is called **_conditioning_**.

Conditioned Response

Behaviorists hold that the _conditioned response_ explains why we do what we do. They say that behavior is learned, shaped, repeated, or curbed by a variety of rewards and punishments in our environment. Put succinctly, people tend to do what is pleasant or rewarding, and tend not to do what is unpleasant or results in punishment. Accordingly, a system of rewards, no rewards, or punishment can be used to bring about, modify, or discourage specific behavior patterns.

Positive Reinforcement

To create a _conditioned response_, a desired behavior is encouraged by pairing it with a reward called _positive reinforcement_. To _condition_ equipment care, for example, every time a student cleans and stores the equipment properly the instructor would respond with positive reinforcement. Positive reinforcement is something desirable or rewarding, such as praise: "You did a very careful and thorough job with the equipment clean-up today, Gabby. Well done. I'm very pleased."

> **INSTRUCTORS TAKE NOTE...**
> • Positive reinforcement is encouraging and stimulates behavior.
> • If a behavior is not positively reinforced, it will extinguish.

The idea is to pair the desired behavior with the "reward" of a compliment. The reward is conditional. It depends on the subject's display of the correct behavior, hence the name _conditioned_ response. The underlying intent, of course, is to encourage Gabby to get in the everyday habit of keeping the equipment clean, neat and orderly. Such regular positive reinforcement encourages regular positive behavior. Positive reinforcement is the corner-stone of motivation, morale and performance.

Extinction

A specific behavior is less likely to occur if it is no longer positively reinforced. Eventually it may cease altogether. In psychology that process is called *extinction*.

If, for example, the instructor never again seems to notice or care about Gabby's hard work in making things shipshape, she may eventually stop putting so much effort into it. Once she no longer perceives any further benefit, she may no longer bother to do it at all. At that point the behavior extinguishes.

Students depend on their instructor to teach them the correct way to perform a task and to convey the need and value of it. An instructor's failure to acknowledge or positively reinforce a student's effort may be perceived by the student as indifference. Indifference, whether real or imagined, on the part of the instructor naturally leads to non-performance on the part of the student; because it implies the task is not very important.

The conditioning process is like a series of small unwritten agreements between instructor and student. "I'll do this if you do that." The student's expectation of repeat reward encourages repeat behavior. If suddenly the reward no longer comes, it signals to the student that the deal is off. The *conditioned behavior* then begins to extinguish. So, to encourage or maintain a student's important behavior patterns an instructor should keep up his/her end of the bargain. *Positively reinforce desirable behavior or risk its extinction.*

> **Extinction -** don't overlook a job well-done or it may not happen again.

Intermittent Reinforcement

After a period of steady conditioning, where reward is *always* given for a desired behavior, sometimes intermittent positive reinforcement may be substituted without risking extinction. For example, in time Gabby may become so accustomed to tidying up the equipment that eventually only occasional praise may be required to inspire her to keep up her good work.

Switching from regular (every time) to intermittent (occasional) positive reinforcement may even become necessary after awhile. After a certain amount of conditioning, positive reinforcement can go stale and lose its appeal. In other words, too much of a good thing is no longer as good.

Gabby could become so accustomed to her daily compliments, for example, that she may begin taking them for granted. As a result, the quality or consistency of her work may start to slip. In such a case it would be better for the instructor to ease up and provide only occasional reinforcement, praising Gabby only when her work is truly exceptional rather than simply good. Switching to an intermittent reinforcement schedule at the right time raises the stakes, restores the perceived value of the positive reinforcement, and leads to improved performance. Intermittent reinforcement is the motivational basis for coaching students and athletes to higher performance.

Self-Reinforcement

In time, certain behavior can become self-reinforcing. An internal motivation develops so the behavior no longer requires outside positive reinforcement. Gabby, for instance, may eventually learn to take independent personal pride in the quality of her work. She may feel good about herself and the neat appearance of her equipment, so she wants to keep it tidy even when no one else is likely to notice. At that point Gabby has developed her own internal positive reinforcement which no longer depends on the instructor's praise. This is an important goal of the instructor's efforts, generating students' self-motivation.

Behavior Modification

For the most part, people are inclined to do what is fun, pleasant or rewarding. Naturally they avoid what is uncomfortable or unpleasant. It's really just common sense.

Though an instructor may use plenty of positive reinforcement to encourage good sailing habits, there are also some negative influences which may be employed to shape, encourage or eliminate certain behaviors. They usually come into play more often when teaching kids than adults. They include:

- **Withholding a positive reinforcement**
  Example: "We will not break for ice cream until everything is shipshape."
- **Removing a negative stimulus**
  Example: "You don't have to do your shore chores today if all the boats are shipshape within 5 minutes."
- **Applying a negative stimulus (punishment)**
  Example: "You have repeatedly neglected your boat, so today you have to organize the sail shed."

Withholding a Positive Reinforcement

Harmful or dangerous excesses in a student's behavior which must be stopped immediately may need to be controlled with instant punishment. For example, if Jake teasingly shoves Abby off the dock, the instructor may issue Jake an immediate stern reprimand to put a quick end to his horseplay.

Avoidance Behavior

A shortcoming of punishment, however, is that it sometimes oversteps its bounds and represses or extinguishes an entire range of otherwise desirable behavior.

A student who has an unpleasant (punishing) experience, such as a capsize, a collision or a crash landing, may later refuse to take the helm again or, worse, give up sailing altogether. Though the only mistake may have been a single momentary steering error, a student may overreact to the past embarrassment by avoiding the entire situation. The student may simply refuse to steer again.

INSTRUCTORS TAKE NOTE...

- Any unpleasantness can be punishing, e.g., extreme temperatures, uncomfortable clothing, an overcrowded cockpit, an uncooperative crewmate, an embarrassing error, a collision, etc.
- Negative experiences can lead to fear, and fear can lead to avoidance behavior.
- A student who develops a sudden headache or complains of nausea may be expressing hidden fear.
- Fear takes the fun out of sailing. When it is no longer fun, the student will eventually stop sailing altogether.

Sailing is a recreational activity. It should be fun. A student's avoidance behavior is a signal to the instructor that the fun is missing and needs to be salvaged. Avoidance behavior is usually the product of fear. So the source of the fear must be identified and addressed.

Fear

Fear can be a serious impediment to learning. It may sometimes go unnoticed and unchecked, because it is often hidden behind avoidance behavior. A student's fear of something, such as heeling, high-wind jibes or docking, can dominate the student's thinking to the exclusion of all else. Because the frightened mind tends to focus on avoiding the fear-producing situation, both memory and reason may be

Behavior Modification

For the most part, people are inclined to do what is fun, pleasant or rewarding. Naturally they avoid what is uncomfortable or unpleasant. It's really just common sense.

Though an instructor may use plenty of positive reinforcement to encourage good sailing habits, there are also some negative influences which may be employed to shape, encourage or eliminate certain behaviors. They usually come into play more often when teaching kids than adults. They include:

- **Withholding a positive reinforcement**
  Example: "We will not break for ice cream until everything is shipshape."
- **Removing a negative stimulus**
  Example: "You don't have to do your shore chores today if all the boats are shipshape within 5 minutes."
- **Applying a negative stimulus (punishment)**
  Example: "You have repeatedly neglected your boat, so today you have to organize the sail shed."

Withholding a Positive Reinforcement

Harmful or dangerous excesses in a student's behavior which must be stopped immediately may need to be controlled with instant punishment. For example, if Jake teasingly shoves Abby off the dock, the instructor may issue Jake an immediate stern reprimand to put a quick end to his horseplay.

Avoidance Behavior

A shortcoming of punishment, however, is that it sometimes oversteps its bounds and represses or extinguishes an entire range of otherwise desirable behavior.

A student who has an unpleasant (punishing) experience, such as a capsize, a collision or a crash landing, may later refuse to take the helm again or, worse, give up sailing altogether. Though the only mistake may have been a single momentary steering error, a student may overreact to the past embarrassment by avoiding the entire situation. The student may simply refuse to steer again.

> **INSTRUCTORS TAKE NOTE...**
>
> - Any unpleasantness can be punishing, e.g., extreme temperatures, uncomfortable clothing, an overcrowded cockpit, an uncooperative crewmate, an embarrassing error, a collision, etc.
> - Negative experiences can lead to fear, and fear can lead to avoidance behavior.
> - A student who develops a sudden headache or complains of nausea may be expressing hidden fear.
> - Fear takes the fun out of sailing. When it is no longer fun, the student will eventually stop sailing altogether.

Sailing is a recreational activity. It should be fun. A student's avoidance behavior is a signal to the instructor that the fun is missing and needs to be salvaged. Avoidance behavior is usually the product of fear. So the source of the fear must be identified and addressed.

Fear

Fear can be a serious impediment to learning. It may sometimes go unnoticed and unchecked, because it is often hidden behind avoidance behavior. A student's fear of something, such as heeling, high-wind jibes or docking, can dominate the student's thinking to the exclusion of all else. Because the frightened mind tends to focus on avoiding the fear-producing situation, both memory and reason may be suspended until the fear passes. The distracting influence of fear can make effective teaching and learning extremely difficult.

Reluctant students who are impassive, who avoid involvement, or who regularly defer certain tasks to others, may actually be avoiding the activity out of fear. It may be a fear of failure, fear of embarrassment, or even fear of some imagined danger. Just as a kid with a burned finger gives fire a wide berth, a sailing student may be reluctant to approach a fear or anxiety producing situation on a sailboat.

INSTRUCTORS TAKE NOTE...
• Don't keep awards a secret. Let your students know about them in advance, so they will have something to strive for.
• Awards motivate best when presented publicly. Peer approval motivates better than keepsakes.
• Award ceremonies motivate best when they are brief and well focused.
• "Praise in public, reprimand in private."

Don't let *fear* replace *learning*.

Instructors need to recognize fear and compensate for it by restoring positive reinforcement to the fearful situation. It requires patience and understanding. Often, working through a trouble-some maneuver side by side with a student, offering encouragement, bolstering self-esteem, and creating a positively reinforcing series of personal successes, will help to allay fear, restore confidence, and rebuild positive motivation.

Motivation

Learning comes much more quickly when a student is comfortable, relaxed, and willing. A student is not simply a passive receptacle for information but an active participant in a learning process. It is a partnership between instructor and student. As in any partnership, willing and earnest teamwork can make all the difference. Willingness stems from motivation, and motivation may stem from a variety of sources.

There are three categories of principal motivating factors:

- Extrinsic rewards
- Intrinsic rewards
- Negative sanctions

Extrinsic Rewards include all of the positive reinforcement which comes from others. They include:

- **Tangible** keepsakes and mementos such as trophies, plaques, diplomas, certificates, prizes, T-shirts, etc.
- **Intangibles** such as approval, praise, compliments, encouragement, admiration, enthusiasm, friendship, or respect of instructors, parents or peers.

Extrinsic rewards are particularly helpful tools when teaching beginners, because beginners need a good deal of initial encouragement. In everyday teaching and coaching, instructor praise and encouragement are the most effective and economical extrinsic awards.

Tangible awards are most effective as a motivator when they are announced *before* instruction begins, rather than after. They should not be kept a secret. The students' hope of winning a prize or getting an award can silently boost their motivation and effort every day.

Extrinsic rewards have a more far-reaching effect when every student stands a realistic chance of winning. If they are few and too exclusive, they have limited appeal as a general motivator. While high achievers certainly deserve their due honors, the runners-up could also benefit from some recognition and formal encouragement. Simple awards or citations, such as "Most Improved," "Shipshape," or

Student Distractions include personal discomforts or preoccupations such as fatigue, illness, pain, hunger, thirst, family problems, uncomfortable clothing, fear or nervousness, a vision or hearing impairment, emotional or physical maladies, and any other personal or private matters which may weigh on a student's mind and compete for attention.

Instructor Distractions include peculiar mannerisms, gestures, or speech patterns, poor hygiene or grooming, inappropriate dress or language, poor attitude, bad manners, or any other attributes which may unnecessarily draw attention away from the intended message

Leadership

The Role of a Role Model

Because an instructor is an authority figure, students are constantly influenced by his or her opinions, judgment, and behavior. It comes with the territory.

Responsible instructors should be quite conscious of the appropriateness of their behavior, so they do not inadvertently set a poor example, and so they can serve as effective role models. Students, particularly younger ones, often want and need role models to set a standard of behavior and performance. If instructors live up to high professional standards, they will naturally earn their students' respect. Once they have their students' respect they are in a position to be effective as leaders, teachers, and coaches.

Leadership Styles

Sailing instructors are as different from one another as sailing students. Each has a unique personality, and each develops a unique personal teaching style. It is important to develop a comfortable and natural style, but be careful to avoid some of the pitfalls. Some instructors adopt leadership styles which serve their own interests better than those of their students.

Authoritarian Style

The Authoritarian Style is characterized by an autocratic and firm attitude. This style is often necessary in situations where the safety of the students, sailors, and boats is at risk. But avoid unnecessary or exaggerated use of this style. You may be perceived as a "Dictator." The *Dictator* is a domineering personality who insists on making all the decisions and giving orders. The Dictator rarely listens to the students or involves them in any decision making regarding their instruction.

Wimp Style

At the other end of the leadership scale is the Wimp Style. The *Wimp* is unsure and submissive and has difficulty making even minor decisions. The Wimp is a pushover who yields too easily in order to avoid conflict. The Wimp may be perceived as spineless for failing to take firm charge when the situation warrants. The Wimp is not well respected by his students, so they do not take his orders seriously.

> The Wimp Style is the opposite extreme from the Authoritarian Style. It shows no leadership control at all.

Cooperative Style

The Cooperative Style of leadership is characterized by teamwork. It is a delicate balance of solid independent leadership and thoughtful student consultation. The Cooperative instructor neither dictates, nor wimps out. The Cooperative instructor encourages student involvement in decision making, listens carefully and fairly, and maintains control without needlessly asserting authority over the students. The Cooperative instructor favors positive leadership skills rather than arrogance or autonomy.

In general, US Sailing encourages instructors to use the Cooperative Style. Nevertheless, they also should be able to shift quickly to the Authoritarian Style when it is the most effective way to safeguard their students' safety. The challenge for instructors is recognizing *when* the Authoritarian Style is justified and necessary, and *how* to avoid overusing it.

Listening Skills

Because teaching is a two-way communication process, where teacher and student provide feedback to one another, listening well is vital. An instructor should listen well, interrupt only to clarify, and pause to think carefully before responding.

> The learning environment must be fun and safe to be effective. Don't let unruly students ruin it for others.

When a student asks a question in a classroom setting, good active listening involves repeating the question for the benefit of the other students who may not have heard, then, after answering, asking if the response fully answers the question. Conscientiously responding to student questions and concerns builds trust and strengthens respect.

Good active listening also sometimes requires discerning the "real message" buried in the words. A student who offers frequent weak excuses, for example, may be masking a totally different hidden concern. Excuses are often indicators of avoidance behavior.

Characteristics of a Leader

Trustworthiness and respect are key ingredients to leadership. A trusted and respected instructor can lift morale and inspire students to outstanding accomplishment. It is only natural for people to want to please or impress people whom they respect or admire.

Conversely, it is only natural for people to be indifferent to those for whom they have no respect. Instructors who fail to live up to their duty as a role model earn little respect from their students. Without the students' respect, motivation suffers, and an instructor can accomplish very little.

Respect does not come automatically with the job title. It must be earned every day. The wise instructor works to earn respect right at the outset of the student/instructor relationship. It is a critical period for developing motivation and good morale.

Students are more apt to accept an instructor's leadership if they feel they are in good hands. That requires some initial trust-building through clearly stated goals, a realistic plan, and an enthusiastic positive attitude.

If you ask students to list the most admirable qualities of people they truly respect, you would hear many of the same characteristics again and again. People respect those who are dedicated, competent, trustworthy, dependable, determined, unselfish, courageous, honest, and have clear and worthy goals and unyielding principles.

If you want to get the job done well, you need to be a good leader. If you want to be a good leader, you have to be trusted and respected. If you want to be trusted and respected, you have to live up to the standards of your duty as a role model. How successful you are largely depends on how well you measure up to the above characteristics.

Taking Charge

An essential duty of any leader is taking charge and giving orders. Students want and need to know what they should be doing. They look to their leader, the instructor, for direction. Students soon lose patience and confidence in leadership which appears confused or uncertain.

> When it's time to take charge, be organized, clear and specific.

Organize yourself *before* class. Have a well defined plan of what you want from a class and then communicate it clearly.

When it is time for decisive action, give direct orders, not suggestions or requests. Direct orders need not be arrogant or abrasive, they simply need to be specific and unambiguous. When it is appropriate to use the Authoritarian style of leadership, use a command voice. Speak simply, clearly, unequivocally, and with a firm command tone. Look your students squarely in the eye when issuing directions. Follow the four W's:

- Who
- What
- When
- Where

> Ambiguity in your choice of words may create confusion between a direct and an indirect command.

Example: "Jake, get a couple of life jacket from the locker; and meet me at the rigging dock in ten minutes."

You cannot expect specific results if your directions are vague and unspecific. "Somebody get a bucket," for example, does not address anyone in particular, so it may get no response at all.

Indirect vs. Direct Commands

Indirect commands are verbal short-cuts. They save the instructor time and words. They may be used as long as the student is appropriately responsive. But if the student appears confused or balks, the instructor may need to revert to simpler direct commands. Beginners often need mostly direct commands until they become accustomed to performing routine maneuvers and are familiar with proper terminology.

- "Pull the tiller toward you" is a **direct command**. A *direct command* requests a simple explicit action without inferring its consequence or intended result.

- "Bear off" is an **indirect command**. An *indirect command* presumes that the student understands what intermediate steps are required (i.e., where to move the tiller) and focuses rather on the intended result.

> ### INSTRUCTORS TAKE NOTE...
>
> **A *direct command*** is very explicit and is appropriate when a beginner is confused or is having trouble understanding technical terms.
>
> **An *indirect command*** is a communication short-cut, useful with more experienced students. It requests a desired result without specifying a method to achieve it.

Team Building

Team building involves building bonds between members of a group. In group instruction it is an important responsibility. The instructor is the group leader and catalyst for student relations. Good morale and a cooperative spirit among classmates can greatly enhance the teaching environment and learning outcome. Break the ice early among new students.

Make introductions right away so that no one feels they are among strangers. Have them engage in games, exercises or social activities which require interaction and cooperation.

Much of the team building process takes place naturally as new students get to know one another. The instructor should be a facilitator not a focal point in the process. Gradually, as familiarity and trust develop, communication, teamwork and morale grow. An instructor should monitor group morale and employ team building exercises as often as needed to keep the learning experience fun and productive.

Discipline

Controlling student misbehavior is not ordinarily an issue when teaching adults, yet it is nearly an everyday occurrence when teaching kids.

Since **safety, fun and learning** are unalterable components of an instructor's mission, no individual student's behavior should be allowed to deprive the rest of the class from reaching these goals.

Preventing Undesirable Behavior

An instructor can prevent most behavior problems by doing three things:

> **INSTRUCTORS TAKE NOTE...**
>
> Some measures to consider in controlling student behavior:
>
> - Prevention
> - Redirection (refocus attention)
> - Extinction (ignore it)
> - Increase responsibility
> - Punishment
> - Suspension
> - Expulsion

1. State clearly and firmly the rules of conduct on the very first day of instruction.
2. Maintain a well structured lesson plan and learning environment.
3. Keep the students busy -- no idle time.

Young sailors with immature social skills, high energy levels, and limited self-discipline generally require more structure in their learning environment than adults. A busy student who is constantly engaged in constructive activity has little time and opportunity to get into mischief. A well-organized and highly constructive daily lesson plan should provide nearly seamless continuity from one activity to the next with very little idle time. When behavior does go awry, it is important that the instructor not overreact and that the response be proportionate to the offense.

Redirection

In mild cases of misbehavior, such as simple inattention, the student may only need to be *redirected*. Redirecting is bringing the errant student to attention and refocusing him or her on the task at hand.

Extinction

Recurring mischievous or disruptive behavior is sometimes an over anxious student's way of seeking the instructor's attention. If so, it is sometimes best handled by extinction, that is, by simply ignoring it. Ignoring the student's antics denies him or her the positive reinforcement of the instructor's attention. Without positive reinforcement the student's undesirable behavior may become less frequent and eventually cease without further action.

Increasing Responsibility

Another technique is to invite a student to assist in conducting the class. Sometimes giving mischievous students some responsibility (such as supervising clean-up, or helping to teach younger students) is all that is needed to instill pride, bring them onto the team, and provide them with needed positive motivation.

Punishment

Harmful or dangerous excesses in a student's behavior, which must be curtailed immediately, may need to be controlled with punishment. Punishment may take the form of a stern reprimand or, in more serious cases, perhaps a suspension of privileges. Chronic misconduct should be brought to the attention of the student's parents, since it may indicate a more deep-seated problem requiring their involvement. See -- "Parents in a Junior Sailing Program" in the *Developing a Program Curriculum* section of this manual for further discussion.

It should be noted that a shortcoming of punishment is that it can cause more problems than it solves by inadvertently extinguishing otherwise desirable behavior. A public reprimand, for instance, may do more than halt childish antics. It may dampen an adolescent's motivation and trigger a defensive response. If an instructor overreacts to the offense, a single minor instance of misbehavior could evolve into an ongoing pattern of withdrawal or defiance. As a rule, punishment should be used sparingly and generally only as a last resort. As the saying goes, "you catch more flies with honey..."

Suspension/Expulsion

Incorrigible and dangerous misconduct which jeopardizes anyone's safety, consistently disrupts the teaching environment, or seriously damages the morale of the other students must be controlled decisively. If a student's persistently unruly behavior cannot be brought under control by one or more of the above measures, it may be necessary to consider suspension or even permanent expulsion.

Verbal Communication

This refers to what you say and how you sound when you say it. There are several key elements:

Using Analogies to Create Learning Bridges

When learning something for the first time, it is difficult to understand the topic without a context or analogies. Effective instructors know that their students will struggle with new material until they gain a point of reference with something they already understand. Providing a learning bridge from what a student already knows to what they are trying to learn may best be accomplished through an analogy. For instance, teaching a young student about apparent wind through the technical explanation of vectors and velocity will be fundamentally confusing. When introducing new concepts, the use of technical terms may lose an audience and create confusion in students. Describing apparent wind to students as the breeze they feel when they ride a bicycle or stick their hand out of the window of a moving car is a connection that nearly all students can comprehend. With a proper description and diagram, students will even understand that the velocity at which the bicycle is moving will affect how much apparent wind deviates from actual ("true") wind. When apparent wind is described as an analogy to something that the students already know that they will be able to grasp what could otherwise be a difficult and technical concept.

Whenever instructors introduce a new skill to their students and they use an analogy, using "like" or "similar to" to provide their students with a connection to something they already understand, they create a bridge that accelerates learning. Explaining that the wind that a bike rider feels is "like" the apparent wind generated by the movement of a boat, or that the velocity at which the bike moves is "similar to" a boat's change of velocity effecting the apparent wind, provides a student with a context for a quick connection to the new material.

When using analogies there is virtually no subject which is too difficult to teach. Everyone has a bank of information stored in their memory which can be used to comprehend new concepts. The instructor's challenge is to know what is in a student's bank of knowledge as the starting point of the bridge. If the instructor assumes an incorrect starting point for the bridge then the analogy, and potentially the lesson, are doomed. As an example, if an instructor of a beginner class for 8 year olds gave an analogy like, "sailing on a reach is like soaring in a glider". While the analogy may be correct, how many 8 year olds have been on a glider, or even know what it is? It would be better for the instructor to find a more common experience for the class to provide and effective learning bridge to make their point.

Voice Quality

Some voices are easy to listen to; others can be quite dull. The quality of an instructor's voice can help or hinder the learning process. Be conscious of the sound of your voice. Do you enunciate clearly so everyone can understand every word? Do you use an appropriate volume, projecting your voice so you can be heard clearly in the back of the room? Does the pitch and tone of your voice vary with enthusiasm and emphasis, or does it remain flat and monotonous?

Pace/Timing

Do you speak too quickly to be fully understood or too slowly to be interesting and hold attention? Nervous novice instructors often speak too quickly. Veteran instructors know the value of slowing down, even pausing now and then for emphasis and assimilation. A few well-chosen words spoken slowly and clearly usually leave a more lasting impression than a breathless stream of unbroken syllables.

Word choice

Big and obscure words are wasted if your students don't understand them. Choose a simple clear vocabulary which everyone can follow. Generally, the simpler a word the better it will be understood. When using nautical terminology or technical jargon, be sure to define each term as you go along. If you are not positive every student recalls terms previously defined, pause to repeat their definition. Some students are understandably shy about speaking up to confess their ignorance of a term. Don't risk losing your audience by carelessly assuming they share your vocabulary.

Avoid verbal excesses such as guttural pauses (e.g. 'urns' and `ers') and stale, trite or overused expressions. They usually distract more than they contribute to the lesson.

Non-Verbal Communication

People unconsciously communicate without words all the time. What people verbalize is only part of the communication process. Non-verbal communication includes everything about you *other than* your spoken words, which contributes to what and how your message is received by your students.

- See yourself as others may see you.
- Is your appearance interfering with learning?

Presence

Your students, almost certainly, will size you up as soon as they first meet you to decide if they are comfortable submitting to your leadership. A confident, deliberate, and enthusiastic appearance will get you started on the right foot. Stand up straight, keep your head up, stay focused, look people in the eye, be well organized, speak clearly, and take charge.

Body Language

How you hold your body can work for you or against you as well. Your posture conveys implied messages about your mood and attitude. Crossed arms or legs suggest defensiveness. A cocked head suggests skepticism or defiance. Leaning forward in a chair or standing too close may suggest assertiveness or aggression. Your total appearance determines how your students will respond to you. For a positive response project a friendly open image. Be body conscious.

Eye Contact

Eye contact is a powerful teaching tool. It not only concentrates and focuses the attention of the student, it supplies the instructor with valuable feedback. Eyes reveal confusion or understanding, excitement or boredom, confidence or insecurity. They tell the instructor when and how to adjust the pace and teaching technique to the needs of the moment. Students need to see your eyes too. They should not be hidden behind sunglasses while classroom teaching. Use sunglasses only in on-the-water instruction.

Attitude

Your facial expressions, body language, tone of voice, general demeanor, behavior, and choice of words all add up to a reflection of your attitude. If it inspires your students, it works in your favor. If it turns them off or disillusions them, it works against you, Think often and carefully about all the subtle messages you send to others about yourself. Remember, you are a role model.

Mixed Signals

Mixed signals are usually the result of carelessness. Mixed signals send opposing messages and create confusion. If you to say, "watch your step," while pointing upwards, a student would not know which way to look, up or down. If you advise your students to use a 3-point stance and step to the center of the hull when boarding, then later you leap onto the bow, your students will notice the contradiction and be confused. Your words and example do not agree. Whether in the classroom or on the water, be sure all of your communication tools are sending a consistent, clear, unambiguous message. Live what you preach every day.

Mannerisms

Mannerisms are behavioral excesses which are usually distracting. They include such nervous habits as pacing, jingling pocket change, tapping a pen, drumming fingers on a desk, or any other repetitive and unproductive behavior. None contribute to the message, and all are distracting to your students.

Gestures

Gestures can work for you or against you. If your gestures are meaningful and clearly help amplify your point, by all means use them. If they are just excess motion or a nervous habit, however, they are a distraction and should be avoided. The eye is naturally drawn to motion. If there is no useful message in your gestures, don't let them draw visual attention away from a more productive part of the lesson.

When to Stop Talking

While some instructors may offer too little feedback to their students, others talk too much. An instructor who talks too much at the wrong time is more of a distraction and a pest than a help.

One such time for an instructor to be sparing with words is during *overload.* A student experiences *overload* when there is too much happening too quickly for the student to assimilate any more input.

During the commotion of a sudden round-up following an accidental flying jibe, for example, is not the best moment for a barrage of feedback. When a student is *fully* occupied with the demands of the moment, feedback probably will not be heard or remembered. Unless there is danger, wait for such a hectic situation to stabilize before beginning instructive feedback.

Curriculum and Lesson Planning

Curriculum Overview

Normally, Level 1 Instructors are not responsible for planning and developing a program curriculum. This is usually done by a program organizer. However, understanding the process will help you to implement the curriculum and prepare lesson plans.

The curriculum for any instructional program is a cursory summation of all courses offered within a program and the major topics covered in each course. Designing a curriculum requires that the planner determine which courses will be offered in a program and then specify their relation to each other. Integrating each sailing course into a cohesive program to enhance program flow is the ultimate goal of curriculum planning. A good curriculum allows a program planner to integrate the subject matter of all the sailing courses to form a logical progression from one course level to the next, emphasizing a **building block** method.

After deciding on the number of classes or courses to be taught and the time frame of each class, the program planner should develop:

- A Syllabus
- Lesson Plans (the course instructor should ultimately take responsibility for writing lesson plans)

When developing or revising a curriculum, it is helpful to get feedback from the students and instructors who were involved in the last course. **To help with future planning, the program director should prepare weekly reports describing how instructors have actually spent their time in comparison to the program plan.** To further aid assessment of the program, instructor's notations on each lesson plan allow insight into the merits and weaknesses of a plan. Record keeping in these areas will help in making adjustments to the curriculum.

Syllabus Overview

The syllabus is either a whole course or weekly list of the topics to be covered in each sailing class. An instructor should use the syllabus:

- to create flow and continuity from class to class, and
- as a broad outline for each lesson plan (including activities for each class).

A smart instructor will create a syllabus for the entire course to properly budget his or her time on each topic or skill and to create a consistent pace for the course.

To develop a syllabus, place all the topics for instruction in your course on a list progressing from basic skills to complex skills. In essence, the list is a sequence of lessons. While each lesson should focus on a specific goal, there should be some overlap in lessons to facilitate a smooth progression from one lesson to the next. Instruction should begin with essential skills (i.e. starting, stopping, tacking) and work toward combining individual skills into a complex skill (i.e. overboard recovery).

Furthermore, a syllabus should organize topic areas so that they utilize the **building block** method of instruction by starting with essential skills and progressing to complex or combined skills. *(See sample syllabus later in this section.)*

Lesson Plan Components

As a starting point for developing lesson plans, refer to the syllabus to locate the topic(s) for the lesson you are planning,

> **Instructors take note:**
>
> A good rule of thumb is one minute of instruction for each year of age of your audience.

then plan activities and methods of instruction that will best convey information to your students. You should try to plan one goal for the day, preparing not more than 2-3 central concepts from that goal. You may find that it is necessary to supply students with supplemental information, or *secondary* concepts, to support the *central* concept(s) of your lesson. The secondary concepts elaborate on, and help to explain the central concepts of your lessons, just like the supporting cast of a play or movie elaborates on the plot. For the enjoyment of your students, keep the pace of different activities lively and use a variety of activities each day. Diversity in your activities will keep students involved and interactive.

There are a number of ways to prepare lesson plans, but whatever format you use it should include the following elements:

- An Objective/Goal
- Student Outcomes
- Materials
- Content
  o Purpose Value Statements or Questions
  o Review
  o Methods/Activities
  o Closure/Review
- Remarks

A PLANNING TIP ...

In a worst case scenario, you may have to delay your detailed planning until you have conducted a couple of classes for assessment of your students.

The Daily Objective/Goal

The daily objective or goal states what specific skill(s) will be taught to students. Remember to keep things simple and limit the number of objectives to attainable levels. Too many goals will end up confusing students.

Measuring Student Outcomes

An instructor measures student's progress in a lesson through student outcomes. Usually, the improvement is measured as a target percentage of students meeting the objective. For example, a stated measurement of student outcomes might read as follows:

100% of the students will successfully conduct a hand pass during a tack, while safely crossing from one side of the boat to the other in moderate to light wind conditions.

Materials

A materials list identifies all the tools an instructor needs to teach their lesson. Be thorough and create a complete and accurate list. How many marks are required? Are there any special teaching tools or props that should go on the list? If the program provides boats, how many will you need? The materials list should be complete enough to pass off to an assistant, either a sailing assistant of parent helper of the day, who can prepare the materials for the lesson and put them where they are needed.

Every student should recognize the purpose and value or a lesson. This will create a higher level of attention towards the lesson.
After the introduction to a lesson, the students should be able to answer the following questions:

- "What is this for?"
- "What good is it?"

Purpose Value Statement or Questions

The purpose value statement or question is a teaching tool. It is a brief opening remark designed to capture the students' attention. Students are more likely to pay attention if they perceive some benefit. So it is helpful when introducing a new topic to begin by stating its purpose and value to the students, or asking a question that accomplishes the same goal. A topic which has no purpose or value need not be in a curriculum. An instructor who cannot clearly state the purpose and value of a subject matter is probably not prepared to teach it.

For example, the following Purpose Value Statement and Question would be effective lead-ins for a presentation on tacking:

Purpose Value Statement

"We will need to learn how to tack today so that once we head out for sailing you will be able to turn around and return to the dock."

Or

Purpose Value Question

"Once we head out to go sailing today, how are you going to turn around to return to the dock?"

While choosing between a statement or question, either for a personal preference or to changing things up, an instructor should opt for whichever format will most successfully engage their students. Write the purpose value statement or question into the lesson plan. Once the attention grabber is complete, an instructor can engage the class in the information of the lesson.

Content

Content is the information and methods an instructor uses to teach a lesson. The content areas are listed below:

Review

As an effective segue into new material, instructors are well served by conducting a brief review of the material or lesson taught at the previous class, or in the lessons that are the building blocks or prior knowledge for the current lesson.

Methods/Activities

Chalk Talks

In the simplest terms, a chalk talk teaches students the theory of a new skill, and how they will practice that skill on the water. A chalk talk starts with a review and the purpose value statement or question.

The lesson should be presented with visual, kinesthetic and auditory methods to reach the widest range of learners. The old adage that a picture is worth a thousand words is particularly true in sailing instruction. Determine the visuals you want to add to your presentation. Draw them in advance and practice how you want them to look. If you have a detailed diagram or lengthy lists, consider preparing a chart in advance to avoid getting bogged down during the presentation. One item that absolutely should be covered during the chalk talk is a description and drawing of the water drills. Once students leave the classroom there should be no ambiguity about what will happen on the water. It should take no more than a sound signal and hand signal to initiate the water drill. Besides feedback, providing detailed instruction or directions on the water is challenging because of environmental conditions and distraction.

For a class of kids, plan on a chalk talk lasting 10 to 15 minutes. Adults can pay attention for 30 to 40 minutes. Classes any longer for their respective audience will absolutely require a kinesthetic activity or the students will likely start drifting off mentally. The other key consideration regarding the age of the class is the language used by the instructor. Remember to talk at an age appropriate level and not over student's heads with technical terms.

In concluding a chalk talk, take some time to conduct an assessment of the student's comprehension. How well have they absorbed the instruction? Using the Discovery method, give the class a "pop-quiz" to determine how well you have taught them. If the student's comprehension is incomplete, the instructor knows what to go over again in the chalk talk stage before finding out on the water that there is a learning error.

Land Drills

Some lessons benefit tremendously from taking the time to conduct a good land drill. A land drill is an important step for learning a skill or understanding a water drill. There are some key elements that make or break a land drill. Be sure to follow the steps below to ensure students perform the drill properly:

1. **Review** the important points from the chalk talk
2. Provide **directions** to the class on what they are going to do in the land drill.
3. **Demonstrate** the land drill to the students.
4. Be sure that every student has an opportunity to **practice** the land drill and receive **feedback** on their practice.
5. **Link** the land drill to the water drill to reduce confusion on the water.

Slow-Motion, Stop-Action, Rewind and Real-Time Drills

The goal of land drills is to move students toward or even into the consolidation phase with fault correction and reinforcement. Demonstrations and land drill offer a very unique opportunity for learning because the pace a student watches and then practices a skill can be controlled. Land drills allow a student to watch a demonstration in slow motion, with stop-action during the most complex elements, and then see the skill performed in real time. At the direction of their Instructor, a student can then practice that skill following the same process allowing for rapid progress from learning phase to consolidation phase. By using different tempos during a land drill, the Instructor allows each student to learn at their own pace. Additionally, an Instructor can really examine a student's progress and assess ability, or identify and correct learning and performance errors more quickly because of the ability to control the pace at which the student practices the skill.

By slowing down a land drill, the Instructor is able to demonstrate multiple facets of a complex skill. For example, in teaching tacking an Instructor could move slowly enough, even stopping at some point, to emphasize and teach the most complicated elements like the hand pass behind the back. When students practice in the land drill, they too can be slowed down or stopped, even back up or rewind to isolate problems or errors for correction.

Once students have had errors corrected, had their comprehension checked, received some positive reinforcement and are able to perform a skill in real-time, they are ready to progress to water drills. Student's practicing a skill in real-time are demonstrating an understanding and ability that directly translates to what they will do on the water.

Skill-Building Land Drills

A skill land drill allows students to practice an actual skill before going out on the water. Examples of this include tacking or jibing in a simulator boat on land. Skill land drills are highly effective for breaking down complex sailing skills into more digestible pieces, or even stop-motion or backing up a skill as student's practice.

Activity Land Drills

Activity land drills are a walk-through of the buoyed course or activity used in a water drill. Activity land drills allow students to practice the course they will sail, reducing the amount of information an Instructor must convey once out on the water. Activity land drills have the added benefit of students sailing the proper course buoyed course sooner, allowing the Instructor to provide feedback earlier. It is advisable that as an Instructor introduces new buoyed courses to a class that they conduct an activity land drill to familiarize students with courses they will use on the water. Once a class has practiced and sailed a course, they will most likely not need to repeat a land drill for the same course.

Consider the following when designing a land drill to make it realistic and effective:

* Be sure that the land drill actually teaches the skill(s) you have as a goal, and that it links the chalk talk and water drill.
* Make the land drill as realistic as possible:
* Use equipment that is as close as possible to what students will use while sailing. If possible, put an actual boat on shore. If that isn't possible, lay out a good representation of the hull with line or tape and use a real rudder and tiller assembly. (See the *Teaching Guide for Sailing Instructors* for examples)
* Use the existing conditions to your advantage. Set things up that take utilize the real wind direction.
* Make sure students use the correct communications and perform steps properly, without taking any shortcuts.
* Keep control of the students who aren't actively doing the drill, and consider ways that they can be passively engaged in the drill such as narrating the action or asking questions.
* Have everyone do the land drill. Provide feedback sandwiches to correct learning and performance errors while providing lots of positive reinforcement.
* The next step will be going out on the water, so having them transitioning from the land drill to the water drill feeling confident about they are going to do will make for a better experience.

Water Drills

The goal of water drills is to improve student's performance errors, not learning errors. If an instructor has to focus on learning errors on the water, then the chalk talk and land drill were inadequate. Many novice instructors rush through the planning phase for water drills, creating drills that don't actually focus of the specified goals in the lesson plan. Some of the most frequent mistakes include;

* Incomplete or misleading directions ashore, or too many directions on the water,
* Incorrect setup of the buoy course,
* Weather conditions exceed the student's ability,

- The instructor focuses feedback on skills other than the goal,
- The instructor positions the powerboat in the wrong location to identify or communicate feedback to students,
- Students have learning errors which should have been caught and addressed in the chalk talk or land drill, or because they are missing key prior knowledge.

No matter the result, the cause is the same, improper lesson preparation. Make sure before you plan the chalk talk and land drill, that the drill(s) you will conduct on the water will actually help students achieve the desired goal.

Here are the keys to success:

1. Make sure the skill practiced in the water drill focuses on the skill being taught,
2. Keep it simple,
3. Take the time to set up the buoy course properly,
4. Using the powerboat, lead students through the first couple of evolutions to make sure they sail the course as designed,
5. Build on success and increase complexity with each successive drill

After the chalk talk and land drill students should be ready and eager for an appropriate drill on the water. After the land drill, give a briefing to the class on where to go and what they will be doing on the water. Any additional directions that the instructor wants to provide are best accomplished before everyone is on the water. Before sending the class out sailing, run through the following checklist to make sure everyone is ready to go sailing:

- Are the weather conditions acceptable?
- Is the powerboat fueled, running and otherwise operational?
- Is the correct gear (marks, visual signals, sound signal, VHF radio, etc.) onboard?
- Is there a rally point where everyone is headed once leaving the dock?
- Does everyone know emergency procedures?
- Does the instructor have a head count of all the boats getting underway?

Games -- Teaching the Fun Way

A good instructor can increase a student's learning progression from practice to automation through the integration of games. As drills become repetitive, the need for practice may still exist, but students begin to experience boredom. The additional stimulus of games allows students to master skills due to their instinct to meet the challenge of the game, rather than focusing on the actual desired skill. Under the guise of games, they can continue to practice without recognizing the old repetitive drills. Their primary focus becomes playing the game rather than concentrating on skills and development. However, turning drills into games can easily become self-defeating if they create performance anxiety.

THE DESIGN OF GAMES SHOULD BE COMPATIBLE WITH A STUDENT'S ABILITY LEVEL and should avoid situations where an individual is compared to other students.

Naturally, the game's design should incorporate the skills being practiced. Map out the game you intend to play before beginning any drills so the overall lesson will follow a more logical progression. You may use land drills as a method of introducing and demonstrating your on-the-water games, or you can have games on land that reinforce sailing knowledge. This will provide sailing students with a fun and entertaining forum, maximizing class time and learning through lesson continuity. US Sailing's publication, *Teach Sailing the Fun Way, is* a good resource for creative activities as well as the "Creative Activities for Sailing Programs" Appendix in the *Small Boat Sailing Level 1 Instructor Guide.*

Key ingredients to "teach the FUN way" include:

1. Present standard material in creative ways -- that rabbit has been coming out of the hole forever! Why not try a new story?
2. Try for 100% group participation.
3. Remember Safety, Fun and Learning.
4. Provide variety.
5. Be prepared -- organize materials that you need ahead of time.
6. Brainstorm with other instructors.
7. Get involved -- the more excited you are, the more fun it will be for the whole group. Remember, you are a role model; and if you are enthusiastic about the activity, your group will be too.
8. Seize the teachable moment -- learning is fun!

Game Possibilities

Team Games		
Team	vs.	Itself
Team	vs.	Performance
Team	vs.	Time
Team	vs.	Team

[Lowest Anxiety]

[Highest Anxiety]

Individual Games		
Individual	vs.	Him/Herself
Individual	vs.	Performance
Individual	vs.	Time
Individual	vs.	Individual

Closure and Review

Once back ashore after the water drills, do not forget to leave some time at the end of the lesson to review present and past topics of study. Allowing a few moments at the end of each class to review the central concept(s) keeps everyone on the same page.

Using the discovery method give the class a verbal "pop-quiz". This provides an excellent summary for the lesson, and reinforces what the students learned. If the Instructor summarizes the day instead of quizzing the students, it is a lost opportunity for students to consolidate information and for the instructor to measure student outcomes. Also, provide some of your overall observations to the class in a group feedback sandwich. Identify skills that the class will continue to practice in the next lesson. Praise individuals for skills they performed well, and spread the praise around from one lesson to the next so every student receives an extrinsic reward, not just the high-flyers. If students leave a class feeling a sense of accomplishment and success, they will be all the more eager for their next lesson.

> **INSTRUCTORS TAKE NOTE...**
>
> As your students improve their skills and if you are setting a starting line, it is important to have your starting buoys square to the wind and spaced an appropriate distance from each other for the number of boats.

Instructor's Lesson Notes

After the lesson, take a few moments to record how the lesson worked. Did it go as you expected? Would you change anything? Did anything important happen with one of your students? Notes addressing these areas will help you make student evaluations at the end of the course and allow the program director to make modifications to the course or curriculum. If you teach that lesson again, the revised lesson plan will help you improve the methods and content of the lesson, avoiding less successful techniques.

Teaching Methods for Physical Skill Building

For new sailing skills, instructors should focus on teaching essential core skills until students are near to mastery before adding lower priority or technical improvements. Educational constructionists emphasize the importance of this building block method of instruction. After learning a solid foundation of skills sailors can add increasingly complex and sophisticated skills to their knowledge base. When instructors introduce, a goal or skill, the design of the lesson should follow a format from which the students will benefit most. The **physical skill building teaching method,** outlined below, represents the progression from a learning phase through the automatic phase to facilitate the learning of new skills.

Step 1 – Chalk Talk and Demonstrations: Theory *Learning Stage*

GOAL: Introduction of a new skill through *classroom chalk talks* with appropriate props, diagrams, role playing and handouts.

The Theory Learning Phase introduces students to new ideas and concepts which may be totally unfamiliar. The "no-pressure" learning environment of a classroom chalk talk presentation or demonstration, with appropriate props, diagrams, role playing, and handouts will allow students to formulate a conceptual or theoretical understanding of the skill or goal. In a chalk talk, students can focus on learning the theory of a new skill. If students were just sent out sailing their boats without benefit of a chalk talk demonstration and land drill, they would struggle with the complexity of learning while sailing the boat in a water drill at the same time. While students may have a strong theoretical understanding after this first stage of a lesson, they will not yet be able to perform the desired skill. Instructors should provide an opportunity for students to learn the theoretical aspect of a new skill before sailing.

Step 2 – Land Drill: Spatial/Physical *Learning Stage*

Even though a student may understand the theory of a new skill or topic, there is no reason to believe that they have developed the physical ability to perform the skill. Sailing skills are often complex and require balance, strength and timing. Land Drills offer students the opportunity to develop a physical understanding of a new theory they have just learned. After building student confidence and knowledge through a land drill, you move on to the next step in your lesson where students now go on the water for actual practice of a skill.

Step 3 – Water Drill: Spatial/Physical *Learning and Consolidation Stage*

GOAL: Practice of physical skills through *Water Drills.*

A Water Drill allows students to merge the smaller segments of a skill (practiced in a land drill) and incorporate them into a complex skill or activity into a complex skill or activity. Remember specific supervision until students are comfortable and capable of executing skills in the water drill.

Step 4 – Games: *Automation Stage*

GOAL: Application of skills through the integration of *games.*

An instructor can then increase a student's learning progression from practice to automation through the integration of games (see "Games -- Teaching the FUN Way" later in this section, the Instructor's Guide, or *Teach Sailing the Fun Way* for more ideas on skill-building games.) Without variety, water drills can become boring and monotonous for students, but most students will try to expand their abilities and excel in a game. The additional stimuli of water games allows students to master skills due to their instinct to meet the challenge of the game, rather than focusing on the actual desired skill. The net result is that students will challenge themselves and push to excel in a game where they might have become paralyzed through analysis by continuing a water drill.

How to Plan a Lesson

As discussed earlier, every lesson starts with a goal and expected student outcomes. As a quick review, the goal is to have students develop a specific sailing (physical) skill. The expected outcomes are the measurement tool to determine your student's success in learning the goal. Use a syllabus to determine what skill(s) to teach in a logical sequence, paced appropriately over the entire length of the course. Then, you can use your syllabus to map out the goals for each lesson you teach.

Many instructors make the mistake of thinking of the chalk talk as the starting point for planning the methods of instruction. This common mistake may be attributed to the fact that a chalk talk is typically the first thing students will do in a class. However, the best place to start planning a lesson is to think through the water drills and work backwards to develop the land drill and chalk talk that will facilitate the water drills. Water drills are the area where students practice actual sailing skills, consolidating and automating the theory they learned ashore. Spend some time developing water drills that will really help students to learn the skills specific to the lesson's goal. If the goal and water drills are known, the instructor has an easier road identifying what land drill best enables the water drills, and what content needs to be covered in a chalk talk to conduct the land drill leading to the water drills. Once these elements are complete, a game on the water can be added to reinforce the students learning process while adding fun to the lesson. Conclude the class with a review on shore and the lesson is complete.

Let's practice making a lesson plan for a 2-3 hour beginning sailing lesson on tacking by setting the following goal and student outcome.

> Objectives/Goals: *Students will learn how to tack from reach to reach, safely and successfully crossing sides of the boat.*

> Student Outcomes: *100% of students will successfully tack from reach to reach and transition from one side of the boat to the other safely and successfully.*

Now that we have a goal and outcome, identify the first water drill for the lesson.

> Methods Activities: Water Drill 1 (20 min.)-*Follow the leader. Switch positions after about 10 min. so everyone gets to practice skipper and crew positions.*

Follow the leader will work well as a first step towards accomplishing the lesson goal, provided we have a second powerboat that can offer feedback to students and assist any struggling students. If you do not have a second powerboat and assistant instructor aboard, consider bypassing this first drill and move directly to the next water drill.

Follow the leader for tacking will allow the instructors to space the boats out, avoid crossing situations, and give the students a target to steer towards while they are learning to tack from reach to reach. Be sure to have skipper and crew changes positions if using doublehanded boats so everyone gets a chance to learn the skills.

Most lessons will have two to three water drills to improve the learning process through increasingly complex practice. Here is the next water drill in our sample lesson for this exercise:

> Methods Activities: Water Drill 2 (30 min.)- *Figure 8 tacking drill.*

A tacking figure 8 water drill will be very effective for sailors practice the skills of tacking reach to reach a little more independently as they start to consolidate the lesson. Instructors in both powerboats can position themselves at opposite ends of the buoyed course to provide feedback to the students.

Having identified a goal, student outcomes and water drills, we can now work backwards to plan what needs to happen in the land drill and water drill that lead up to water drills.

Methods Activities: Chalk Talk Review (5 min.)- Review through Discovery method the following topics we have covered:

-   Wind direction
-   Steering
-   Where to sit
-   Safety concerns (ducking boom)
-   Points of sail/Sail position
-   Communication

Methods Activities: Chalk Talk Purpose Value Statement (2 min.)- Ask the following question:

"So now that you know how to start and stop, once you leave the dock and sail away, how will you return to come back again?"

Methods Activities: Chalk Talk Presentation (10 min.)- Based on responses to the PVQ;

1. Write "Tacking: How to turn around" on the board.
2. Describe what a tack is, list 4 steps for tacking, and draw diagram of maneuver.
    1. Look before you tack
    2. Communicate before turning
    3. Tiller toward sail and duck
    4. Straighten tiller when turned around
3. Show mirror image if boat starts on opposite tack.
4. Ask for questions on 4 steps to gauge student comprehension.
5. Describe the class's on-the-water rendezvous spot for leaving and returning to the dock.
6. Diagram and describe Water Drill 1: Follow the Leader.
7. Using existing illustrations of boats tacking, diagram and describe Water Drill 2: Tacking Figure 8. Caution about crossing zone and using Tiller Towards Trouble.

Methods Activities: Land Drill: Simulate Tack in boat on shore (25 min.)- Provide Directions, Demonstrate, have students practice, provide feedback to each student. Practice until 100% of students perform skill correctly.

Methods Activities: Rigging (20 min.)- Aid and assist all sailors in properly rigging boats. Once the lead instructor is afloat on powerboat, push class off dock, boat by boat to rendezvous spot.

Methods Activities: Unrigging (20 min.)- Aid and assist all boat in landing safely, boat-by boat and not whole group at one time. Be sure all equipment is put away properly.

Methods Activities: Closure Review (5 min.)-

1. Through Discovery method, review the following topics covered in this lesson:
    -   4 steps of tack
    -   Definition of tacking
2. Present skill areas that the group performed well
3. Present skill areas that we will continue to work on
4. Compliment class for successfully learning to turn around

Next, we will look at the final version of this sample lesson plan, with all of the methods in their correct spot:

Class: Beginner 420's

Objectives/Goals: Students will learn how to tack from reach to reach, safely and successfully crossing sides of the boat.

Student Outcomes: 100% of students will successfully tack from reach to reach and transition from one side of the boat to the other safely and successfully.

Methods Activities: Chalk Talk Review (5 min.)- Review through Discovery method the following topics we have covered:

- Wind direction
- Steering
- Where to sit

- Safety concerns (ducking boom)
- Points of sail/Sail position
- Communication

Methods Activities: Chalk Talk Purpose Value Statement (2 min.)- Ask the following question:

"So now that you know how to start and stop, once you leave the dock and sail away, how will you return to come back again?"

Methods Activities: Chalk Talk Presentation (10 min.)- Based on responses to the PVQ;

8. Write "Tacking: How to turn around" on the board.
9. Describe what a tack is, list 4 steps for tacking, and draw diagram of maneuver.
    1. Look before you tack
    2. Communicate before turning
    3. Tiller toward sail and duck
    4. Straighten tiller when turned around
10. Show mirror image if boat starts on opposite tack.
11. Ask for questions on 4 steps to gauge student comprehension.
12. Describe the class's on-the-water rendezvous spot for leaving and returning to the dock.
13. Diagram and describe Water Drill 1: Follow the Leader.
14. Using existing illustrations of boats tacking, diagram and describe Water Drill 2: Tacking Figure 8. Caution about crossing zone and using Tiller Towards Trouble.

Methods Activities: Land Drill: Simulate Tack in boat on shore (25 min.)- Provide Directions, Demonstrate, have students practice, provide feedback to each student. Practice until 100% of students perform skill correctly.

Methods Activities: Rigging (20 min.)- Aid and assist all sailors in properly rigging boats. Once the lead instructor is afloat on powerboat, push class off dock, boat by boat to rendezvous spot.

Methods Activities: Water Drill 1 (20 min.)-Follow the leader. Switch positions after about 10 min. so everyone gets to practice skipper and crew positions.

Methods Activities: Water Drill 2 (30 min.)- Figure 8 tacking drill.

Methods Activities: Unrigging (20 min.)- Aid and assist all boat in landing safely, boat-by boat and not whole group at one time. Be sure all equipment is put away properly.

Methods Activities: Closure Review (5 min.)-

1. Through Discovery method, review the following topics covered in this lesson:
    - 4 steps of tack
    - Definition of tacking
2. Present skill areas that the group performed well
3. Present skill areas that we will continue to work on

4. Compliment class for successfully learning to turn around

Other Considerations for Successful Lesson Planning

The three most important objectives in creating a curriculum and subsequent lesson plans are **SAFETY, FUN and LEARNING.** Safety and learning are obvious, but all too often fun is left out. Designing a course that includes fun is not only more enjoyable, but also enhances and facilitates learning (See "Games --Teaching the Fun Way" in Section 2). In other words, most people learn best when they don't even realize that they are learning, but are merely enjoying an activity. Several keys to a fun and successful sailing course are:

Time Allocation and Lesson Planning

The most important aspect of time allocation and lesson planning is making sure that you do not try to cover too much information. If you create a schedule where the students must absorb more than 2-3 primary concepts per class, you will probably be teaching over their heads and beyond their ability. This is especially true of beginning sailors where *every* skill and idea is new to them. Keeping things simple in the allocated time will allow more students to master skills and information so they will feel successful and want to learn more.

Diversity

Repetitive activities soon become boring and dull. By teaching through varied activities you will keep classes fresh and exciting.

Organization and Preparation

There are few things that are more frustrating than a lack of organization. Not only does it appear unprofessional, but loose ends and complications make the learning process more difficult for all students. This is why US Sailing advocates using the building block method of instruction. The *building block method* is where each course and each lesson are linked together to maximize flow and continuity in subject matter. Prior planning is absolutely essential for efficient integration of subject matter.

Demonstrations

"Showing them what you mean" is a critical element of effective teaching. It sets a visual standard of performance for students to imitate. Students often imitate what they have seen rather than do what they were told. So it is important to conduct all demonstrations properly, "by the book."

Diagram a water drill on shore, and even walk through a land drill simulation of the water drill, before heading out on the water. Do not cut corners or take liberties with standard procedures. It may only instill bad habits you will have to correct later.

Pace

To simplify your task, research previous lesson plans and student evaluations as a guideline and reference. In general, strike a balance between going slow enough for everyone to master a skill and rushing ahead so quickly that students don't understand how to perform the skills. In teaching skills correctly the first time, you will not necessarily be able to guarantee that every student can actually perform the skill. Rather, each student should understand *how* to perform the skill and understand the areas they need to improve for mastery of the skill. It is, however, more important to give beginning students more time to learn and master basic skills before progressing to more advanced skills and catering to advanced students.

Local Conditions

You must also take into account prevailing weather patterns.

Is it light wind in the morning building up to a fresh breeze, or the reverse? If your sailing site is tidal and you can only sail so many hours around high tide, that too must be considered. You have to decide when it is best to schedule each class so that students can maximize their learning time by practicing during weather conditions within their abilities.

Class/Session Time

Instructors are most often assigned a block of time for the class(es) they with instruct. Remember that a large portion of class time is going to be taken up with rigging boats and getting to the sailing area. When planning the activities in lessons, take into consideration:

• The attention span of the students

• The difficulty of the skills students will be learning

• The goals and activities of each lesson

• Other activities and obligations of your students

Imagination and Innovation

There are many effective methods for teaching a subject. An instructor must take into account his or her own teaching strengths and weaknesses, and more importantly the needs of the students. Dare to be creative. Very often the best lessons are those that are completely unique from any other. Additionally, most people develop a better understanding of new material if they can relate it to something they already understand. If you can help students to make such connections, your job will be easier. Consider the best and most memorable lessons you have had. Why are those lessons so lasting in your memory?

Remember that your lesson plans must be detailed enough for other instructors to use. In the event that you are unable to teach a class (i.e. field trips, other activities or duties, illness) another instructor will probably have to take your place, just like a substitute teacher. A complete and detailed class plan will keep your class outline on target and produce the goals you set when you wrote the lesson.

SAMPLE: LESSON PLAN

LESSON PLAN FOR: _____   **DATE**:_____

LESSON NUMBER: _____

OBJECTIVE/GOAL:

MATERIALS:

CONTENT REVIEW:

NEW MATERIAL:

METHODS ACTIVITIES:

(min.)

(min.)

(min.)

(min.)

REVIEW/CLOSURE:

(min.)

INSTRUCTOR'S LESSON SELF-ASSESSMENT

Teaching Sailors with Disabilities

One of the most noble, challenging, and rewarding experiences you may have as a sailing instructor is to teach students with disabilities. As sailing instructors we find many extrinsic rewards. However, *the greatest reward that we all take from our job is the development and growth of our students.* Watching the progress of our pupils from day to day, all the way through to year after year is the single most rewarding aspect of sailing instruction. By identifying proper goals, and developing lessons to achieve those goals, an instructor can assist students in achieving and excelling in areas thought unattainable.

Imagine teaching a visually impaired sailor to detect, react and adjust to wind shifts, or assisting a paralytic student to gain self-sufficiency in the boat. Perhaps your work as an instructor can aid students with learning disabilities, from Dyslexia to Attention Deficit Disorders, to develop coping mechanisms through their sailing which they can then apply to their lives ashore. The only boundaries to which a good sailing instructor adheres are SAFETY, FUN and LEARNING.

Often, the greatest concern for sailing instructors is getting started. Questions like, "How should I design my classes?", "Do I have to teach differently?" and "Where should I begin?" are all solved with one answer. *Design and teach classes the same way you would in any setting -- BUT ALSO be sensitive to the students' needs!* Special consideration may be necessary for such things as: braces and prosthetic devices, the dexterity of students, medications, loss of control or epilepsy, sanitation and bathrooms, etc.; but the fundamentals of teaching sailing still apply.

1. Assess your students' ability levels.

    When instructing students with physical disabilities or learning disabilities, you must assess not only what their sailing abilities are but also where their disabilities might prove harmful during instructional or sailing situations. You must also know your students' abilities for you to teach at the proper pace and ability level.

2. Understand your students' learning styles.
    In any teaching situation, you will be most effective when you can teach to the predominant learning styles of your students.

3. Set goals with your students, not for your students
    Whenever you set goals, it helps to identify easily attained short term confidence building goals as well as more complex long term goals. A building block approach facilitates this type of student growth.

4. Set class size limits to reflect the desired teacher-to-student ratio
    When teaching disabled students who will progress at notably different speeds, it is essential to keep the teacher-to-student ratio very low to provide the necessary individualized attention. The more individualized attention a student requires, the fewer students you should have in the class competing for the instructor's attention.

Your efforts to ensure that classes for disabled students are safe and effective will require **more thorough planning.** You must also educate yourself as much as possible about your students' disabilities so that you can better understand how to help them through the rigors of sailing instruction. While explaining and describing all the possible situations a sailing instructor may have to solve is impossible, the following will help you to make initial decisions, develop a framework of instruction, and introduce you to core strategies and concepts for teaching.

Teaching Sailors with Physical Disabilities

Assessing Physical Disabilities and Essential Functions

In July, 1990, the *Americans with Disabilities Act* (ADA) was signed into law prohibiting discrimination based on disabilities. The ADA requires all affected entities to provide **"reasonable accommodation"** for persons with disabilities. In short, this means that sporting programs must provide opportunities for participation in activities to qualified individuals. Developing a method for reasonable accommodation requires that you know what is required of a "qualified" individual, and what can be considered a "reasonable" accommodation.

To begin, you must make some key assessments of:

1. your **facilities and equipment**,
2. your **students' functional abilities** which must be jointly determined with your students (and their parents/legal guardian(s) if applicable), and,
3. **essential functions required** to actively participate in sailing.

Pause for a moment to consider what essential functions (such as pulling/pushing, paddling) there are in the sport of sailing.

Depending on equipment availability and instructor assistance, **there are few functions that could prevent a disabled student from participating in sailing.** Even communication barriers, one of the most critical functional areas on the water, can usually be overcome with some minor training modification and

> **AN IMPORTANT ESSENTIAL FUNCTION...**
>
> Don't forget that swimming and comfort in the water are required for all students!

accommodation. Your sailing program directors and instructors should create a detailed list of the essential functions for sailing. Make sure that you can communicate and defend your definitions. Finally, you should assess whether participation is affected if one essential skill cannot be performed. For instance, if a student cannot swim, and does not feel comfortable in the water, is your sailing program or class able to develop a reasonable accommodation for that student? One such modification would be allowing the student to wear the PFD during the swim test.

Adequate Functionality

The next step is for the student and instructor/program directors to determine whether a disability will affect performance and require reasonable accommodation. Your program must address issues of accessibility to your facility, docks, boats and equipment in determining reasonable accommodations. This determination should *never* be made without a consultation with the student. **Students should be asked whether they can perform functions or describe the reasonable accommodation they would require.** Students with physical disabilities will require substantially different accommodations and attention. Discuss with the student if they think they are functionally accommodated by the proposals you are able to devise. The final decision for participation should be determined by whether or not your program can provide reasonable and adequate accommodations for a student.

Access to the Program

Readily achievable barrier removal

Public accommodations are required to remove barriers only when it is "readily achievable" to do so. "Readily achievable" is defined as something that is easily accomplishable and able to be carried out without much difficulty or expense.

How does the "readily achievable" standard relate to other standards in the ADA? The ADA establishes different standards for existing facilities and new construction. In existing facilities, where retrofitting may be expensive, the requirement to provide access is less stringent than it is in new construction and alterations, where accessibility can be incorporated in the initial stages of design and construction without a significant increase in cost.

It's in a program's best interests to consider making "readily achievable" modifications to its existing facilities. Working in conjunction with knowledgeable people with and without disabilities can greatly assist in devising and designing workable and safe solutions to existing barriers to active participation.

For example, in areas where there is a significant tidal shift, steep ramp inclines are a hazard to everyone. Other concerns include the width, freeboard, and stability of floating docks and finger piers. Is there ample and appropriate parking? If you can't get your student safely to the boats, you can't teach them to sail.

Independent Transfer

As you can understand, safely boarding vessels can be tricky and possibly injurious for both the student and the instructor. Some students are extremely independent and may want to transfer themselves into the boat. While this is a desirable goal, as the instructor it's your responsibility to be sure the transfer is conducted safely.

1. Does the student have an **adequate life jacket?**
2. Has the student ever **transferred** before?
3. Does the student require **special attention** to get into a boat?
4. Does the student have sufficient strength for an independent transfer into a boat?
5. Can the **boat be firmly attached to the dock?** Increased stability is often obtained by letting the bow line out and bringing the stern in close to the dock, then resnugging the bow line.
6. If the transfer is to the dock, are there **splinters?** If so, what can be done to protect the student?

Assisted Carries

If a student does not have the physical strength or the confidence to try an independent transfer, an **assisted carry** is an option for transferring a student into the boat. Be sure to ask the student if a carry is acceptable to him/her. Often, a student will have a preferred method which will keep him/her most comfortable. Some factors to consider when performing a carry include:

- Remember, always ask your students if they would like your assistance **before you** assist them!
- **Have a plan** as to how you will conduct a carry.
- **Practice** before attempting an actual carry. You may be surprised by the unforeseen complications involved!
- Determine how the student is to be picked up (hands/wrist/legs, cross chest/armpits/legs, support legs, etc.).

- Discuss all details of the carry with the student.
- Have **spotters** positioned in case lifter(s) lose their balance.
- Use **cushions** to prevent injury on the dock.
- Have the student give the "ready, set, go!"
- Always bend at the knees, using your **legs to lift** and keeping your back straight!

Prevention of Sailing Related Injuries

In addition to wanting sailing facilities that are accessible and safe, all students have some concerns about sustaining injuries while involved in physical activities. Students with a lack of sensation can be injured or receive pressure sores without their knowledge.

- Proper Facilities
- By following some basic preventive measures, you can provide a safer environment for all students:
- Pad all exposed sharp or abrasive areas.
- **Provide a stable area** in the boat for those students concerned with losing their balance.
- **Keep lines** running into the cockpit area **tangle free** and as uncluttered as possible.
- Acquaint students with the operation of equipment on the boat that could cause injury, such as blocks, clamps and the boom.
- **Discuss the boathandling characteristics** of the sailboat you will be using so there are no surprises. Discuss the stability of the boat, its seating, lines and what happens during maneuvers like tacks and jibes in various wind conditions.

Proper Clothing

The old adage, "It's easier to take off something you don't need, than to put on something you didn't take," is perhaps the best advice in preparing to go sailing. Layering is the proven method of dealing with temperature changes. Some individuals are unable to naturally retain heat or perspire; although others may not. As their instructor you will be responsible for helping your students to remain safe and comfortable and provide adequate assistance.

> **A CAUTIONARY NOTE...**
>
> Temperature related emergencies progress rapidly for some students with physical or developmental disabilities. They may not be able to feel when they are getting too hot or too cold.

Symptoms for heat related emergencies are the same for people with disabilities. However, the onset of an emergency may come more quickly for a sailor with disabilities. Prevention of heat emergencies is the same, though. Drinking plenty of liquids (water is best), having a spray bottle at hand, and keeping skin protected from the elements and the direct effects of the sun will combat injuries.

Poor circulation and lack of muscle movement can rapidly bring on a case of hypothermia. As with any student, the instructor should take preventive measures prior to the student taking to the water. Always be prepared for temperature changes.

Life jackets

US Sailing requires all candidates taking a US Sailing Instructor Course to wear life jackets whenever they are *near or on* the water. This policy is highly recommended for *all* students at *all* other times, and it is a good idea to enforce this safety rule regardless of the students' level of swimming ability. Now is the time to establish safety habits that last a lifetime!

Proper type and fit of the life jacket are the responsibility of the instructor. If your program or the student provides the life jacket, test fit the life jacket under controlled conditions (in a pool for instance) prior to the start of instruction. For individuals with mobility limitations Type I or Type II life jackets provide the greatest degree of flotation.

Capsize Recovery

Capsize recovery is an essential skill taught to *all* students. When introducing any student to why capsizes occur, explain that this is normal in certain types of sailboats, and then explain how to properly right the boat. Since you've already determined the students' comfort level in the water, taking the next step to capsize recovery should be relatively easy.

> **A SAFETY POLICY...**
>
> If a student cannot right a capsized boat independently, he or she should not sail solo until a method of capsize recovery is mastered.

Again, patience is a major factor. Some physically stronger students will quickly right the boat (within 1 to 2 minutes), while others require more time (students with weak upper body strength can take as long as 35 minutes) to complete the exercise. **Give students adequate time to figure out a method that works for them, but be on guard against hypothermia. Not** everyone will be able to execute a solo scoop recovery.

Risk Management, Liability and Safety

Section 4 in this manual covers the subject of risk management and liability. As the instructor, it's your responsibility to clearly explain the risks involved in sailing to all your students (and parents/guardians when applicable). By getting everyone's concerns into the open, and understanding the inherent dangers in sailing, a final decision about participation can be agreed upon. Once informed of potential risks, it's the student's right (with parental/guardian consent when applicable) to continue with the course of instruction. This mutual understanding of the risks and steps necessary to reduce risks will go a long way toward insuring a safe and enjoyable experience for everyone.

Safe practice and teaching methods are the foundation of US Sailing program of instruction. This does not change when teaching individuals with disabilities

Teaching Sailors with Learning Disabilities

Earlier in this manual we discussed how people learn and recognized that everyone learns differently. All people have strengths and weaknesses in terms of how they learn, and/or how they process information. It is becoming more common to have students who have been diagnosed with Autism, Specific

> **INSTRUCTORS TAKE NOTE...**
>
> Often, people will hesitate to inform you of a disability to avoid the stigma attached with special needs. It is important to realize that **students with disabilities don't want to be treated any differently;** they just want to participate like anyone else.

Learning Disability, or other disabilities recognized by the Individuals with Disabilities Education Act (IDEA). Injuries such as Traumatic Brain Injury (TBI) also result in learning challenges, and manifest one or all of the following learning areas. Be aware that many students will exhibit some of the characteristics of a learning disability although they have not been diagnosed. Teaching these sailors will require you to refine the teaching skills you have learned.

It is important to understand your students. If you have ever been in a situation where you "spaced out," couldn't understand verbal directions or struggled with a written passage, you have experienced what a student with learning disabilities copes with every day. You can control when you daydream while a person with Attention Deficit/Hyperactivity Disorder (AD/HD) has much more difficulty remaining focused. For you processing information, reading and writing do not require the extra time and effort that a student with learning disabilities needs to comprehend information and complete tasks.

Characteristics of learning disabilities may include some of the following, but are not limited to:

- ❑ Short attention span
- ❑ Restlessness
- ❑ Impulsiveness
- ❑ Organizational difficulty
- ❑ Difficulty reading or comprehending written materials
- ❑ Difficulty understanding and following verbal directions and information
- ❑ Difficulty starting and finishing projects
- ❑ Relational difficulty
- ❑ Spatial difficulty
- ❑ Easily-triggered anger
- ❑ Negative internal feelings and self-image
- ❑ Low energy
- ❑ Normal or above average IQ
- ❑ Very messy handwriting

While the symptoms of some learning disabilities can be treated with medication, you, as an instructor, must also take measures to accommodate students with learning disabilities. If students exhibit several of these symptoms, you may want to contact their parents/guardians for some suggestions on teaching and behavior management techniques. Be careful not to assume or imply that the student has a diagnosed learning disability.

Class size, structure, rules, plans and activities must all be adjusted to accommodate students with learning disabilities. In many cases, students with learning disabilities will not require substantial accommodations because they have been able to develop coping mechanisms which allow them to function at a higher level.

Due to the nature of learning disabilities characteristics, an instructor's teaching style must take into consideration the learning needs of his or her students. Review the list of symptoms mentioned earlier. What alterations would you make to accommodate a student with learning disabilities?

Class Size

Depending on the severity of a learning disability, some students may require one-on-one instruction while other students with learning disabilities may be able to function in a large class without any accommodation. Individual assessments and the students' development of coping mechanisms will be the greatest determining factors for how much attention is required by their instructor. However, don't forget that for most sailors an integral part of the sport is socializing. It will be important for all students to have a social aspect to their lessons. Tutorial lessons alone could further stigmatize a student who has problems with self-confidence.

Teaching Style

Students will function better in kinesthetic class situations compared to auditory or visual situations largely because of the level of stimulation provided. Teaching a student with learning disabilities without primarily using a kinesthetic approach will come up short. Repetition and review, while introducing new topics, will help students with learning disabilities develop confidence. Reinforcing a student's knowledge base and areas of security will help students with learning disabilities to progress. Focusing on core content areas until mastery and automation will also allow students with learning disabilities to confidently progress.

Some general communication techniques are:

- Adjust your language level if you need to by using simpler words or shorter phrases.
- Be aware that the student may have a narrower scope of interests and less motivation to engage socially.
- Ask yes or no questions instead of open-ended ones.
- Be more concrete and literal with your language.
- Students often miss subtle cues (like tone of voice), and they may interpret metaphors and sarcasm literally.
- Engage the student by finding out a specific likes or dislikes of the student and ask them about it.
- Be patient with the student's handling of conversational topics. It may be difficult for the student to understand that you aren't as fascinated by a particular area of interest as he or she is.

- Don't misinterpret a lack of eye contact as inattention or rudeness. Eye contact may actually hinder comprehension on the student's part.
- Be aware of the potential distractions. You're student may fixate on something you barely notice.

Reinforcement

Students with learning disabilities are often lacking in self assurance. They may question their competency in areas where you know they are qualified. **Such students with learning disabilities not only enjoy praise for their good work, but also need it to build their self-confidence.** The feedback sandwich should probably be modified slightly for students with learning disabilities to provide more positive reinforcement. Be honest with praise and never sarcastic. Sarcasm could be misinterpreted as a personal attack and false praise will be detected; both of which will cause students to lose self-confidence and respect for you.

Routine

Developing a pattern or standard method of operation is essential for students with learning disabilities. Consider for a moment what is involved with change. Change requires that a student learns a new set of rules, a new method of operation. For the student with a learning disability deviating from a routine can be confusing and thus discouraging. New directions that are given just verbally may be difficult for students with learning disabilities to process and understand. As you set down rules or instructions, make sure to convey information through multiple methods. Write down the instructions, read and discuss the instructions with students, provide time for an actual demonstration of new procedures (if appropriate), have students actually repeat the new instructions and review the rules.

Lesson Plans

Lessons must be created that keep students active and involved. Idle time is an opportunity to become distracted and/or "space out." **Design lessons that focus on achievable goals.** Students with learning disabilities do *not* benefit from lessons in which they fail. Additionally, **review and reaffirm skills you are teaching.** For instance, after a thorough whiteboard description of an on-the-water drill, have students draw the course on a piece of paper, and then walk through a land drill before hitting the water. Each stage of introducing material, from theory, to concept, to spatial/physical comprehension, to practice allows a student to be successful. (See "Teaching New Skills" in Sections 1 and 2).

Testing and Evaluation

Assessing students with learning disabilities for their knowledge and ability through traditional testing methods will not reflect their true capabilities. Identify what you are truly testing - recall ability or comprehension. Providing the time a student needs to complete a test, not a time limit, will infinitely increase their success on exams. However, open book evaluations and demonstrations of ability may be more appropriate assessment methods for students with learning disabilities. Due to difficulties in written expression, you may find that verbal evaluations allow a student with learning disabilities to convey information more freely. Remember, sailing is supposed to be FUN!

Discipline

Cause and effect often elude students with learning disabilities. **Providing a highly structured but fair set of rules for behavior and conduct can alleviate discipline concerns.** In fact, create the rules with your students and the rules will carry even more emphasis because the students set their own limits. The old stand-by of "firm, but fair" never had a greater role than in dealing with challenging behavior. Students with learning disabilities retain and repeat things literally. Therefore, say what you mean and mean what you say in both discipline and teaching situations.

Conclusion

Instructing students with learning disabilities won't be much different than any other sailing class. Instructors must simply be *more thorough in planning and designing lessons, and patient in their teaching*. In fact, looking at the demographics of any class will illustrate that you have and will be working with students with a variety of abilities and disabilities. Out of 20 students in a class, you can expect that:

> 70% (14 students) could be predominantly **visual** learners
> 25% (5 students) could be predominantly **auditory** learners
> 5% (1 student) could be a predominantly **kinesthetic** learner
> 60% (12 students) could be **visually impaired**
> 30% (6 students) could have a **learning disability**
> 15% (3 students) could have **Dyslexia**
> 5% (1 student) could be **colorblind**

In general, teaching students with disabilities could be the most rewarding challenge encountered by an instructor. There is no greater opportunity to participate in the triumph of the human spirit. **In preparing yourself to teach students with disabilities, you will need to understand your students' abilities and disabilities, patiently support their progress, look to create solutions to seemingly impossible situations, and identify with your students.** After all is said and done, the extrinsic and intrinsic rewards you receive will be well worth the efforts you undertake. Prepare yourself to be amazed!

ADDENDUM

TEN STEPS OF RISK MANAGEMENT FOR SAILING INSTRUCTORS

As a sailing instructor, there are a number of precautions that you, along with those who arrange and supervise a sailing program, can take to try to ensure a safe program. Using this approach will give you a good foundation for satisfying many of your legal duties. Let's look at each of these in some detail.

1: Plan your program thoroughly.

Using materials from US Sailing, from prior programs of your sponsoring organization, and from your own experience, develop a complete program of instruction. **Individual lesson plans for each week, and even each day, will be important to the overall continuity of instruction, incorporating the preferable sequence of teaching specific skills, from basic to advanced.**

The program should also **make provision for individual evaluation of each student.** Rate them frequently, discuss their progress, and be prepared to modify your instruction plan to adapt to their progress. **Progress should be recorded in a WRITTEN DOCUMENT** available to students, families, and your sponsoring organization.

2: Assess risks on a continuing basis.

Go back to basic risk evaluation, review and discuss each type of possible risk with your sponsoring organization and staff before your program starts. **Record** each risk and the suggested response to it, making sure that each response is prudent, practical and affordable. Then set responsibilities for assuring that these risks are continually reassessed, in light of new conditions, and that your students and their parents are aware of the risk control standards that have been adopted.

A **Participation Agreement** signed by each student (or a parent/guardian if appropriate) should be on file before classes begin. In these documents prospective sailing students acknowledge that they understand the *inherent dangers* involved with sailing (like capsizing, drowning, head injuries, crushed fingers, etc.) and yet are willing to assume these risks by indicating that they want to participate in a sailing class. Signs, orientation meetings and films are also ways to inform prospective sailors about the *inherent dangers* of sailing. The constant repetition of rules and cautions may be annoying, but it will, in the long run, create the appreciation of risk and prudence that will prevent accidents.

SAMPLE NOTIFICATION WARNING STUDENTS ABOUT POLLUTED WATERS... "The sailing lessons will be given in the waters off (name of sailing center). These waters have been stated to be polluted. All of our instructors have been trained in these waters and in that regard immersed in them on numerous occasions without ill effect. However, there is a risk for any person who comes in contact with these waters and that risk should be clearly known and understood by all participants, parents and/or guardians. In our sailing program or any other similar program, it is inevitable that students come in contact with the water and thereby are exposed to its risks. Any student who falls into the waters will be rinsed with clean water as soon as practicable thereafter -- the optimum that can be done in these circumstances."

3. Understand the capabilities and limitations of your students.

Swimming is the first and most important capability for any student. There is no substitute for a **swimming test.** Next, the program should assure the physical fitness of each student for the sailing regimen, including a complete written health statement from a responsible person, with any limitations or special medical conditions noted that could affect participation. If in doubt, ask questions. If a student returns to the program after an injury or illness, a physician's statement may be required. Finally, you should understand the prior sailing experience of each student so that he or she may be placed in the appropriate level of instruction.

4. Provide and maintain a safe physical environment.

First check the land-based location from which you will be operating. Are the grounds, buildings, and docks safe for your students and their activities? Under the law you are responsible for both *actual* and *constructive* knowledge of an unsafe condition. Anything you should have discovered in a regular inspection will be deemed constructive knowledge for which you are still liable. *Actual notice* occurs when the responsible party is given notice of an unsafe condition. To perform your duty, you must provide notice, both *actual notice* and *constructive notice.*

Waivers and **"Release of Liability"** forms have been very popular for the last several years. Although not always successful at avoiding liability, they have been very effective in providing both actual and constructive notice. Because these types of forms need to be customized to conform with each state's laws and regulations, we recommend that each facility/organization's attorney draft a release form that provides actual and constructive notice for their situations. Make sure that a parent or guardian signs these forms, if you are teaching underage kids.

Then review the waters in which you will be sailing. Are they safe to swim in? Can pollution conditions change? Are floats and moorings safe and inspected periodically?

Facility Inspection Guidelines are an essential component of any safe sailing program and will help to prevent accidents. Conduct inspections each day and each week and keep a record of findings, actions taken to reduce risks and warnings given about inherent risks. Nearby electrical wires, planking with splinters, sharp edges, exposed nails and similar hazards should be noted and immediate corrections made. If there is a chance of periodic water pollution, learn how to take daily tests -- don't depend on public authorities to warn you.

Finally, since weather conditions can and will change quickly, listen to radio weather forecasts and be prepared to respond to new conditions. If a squall threatens, you should take your students off the water immediately.

5. Provide and maintain proper equipment.

Your program depends on the continued availability of equipment, owned by you, your sponsoring organization, and/or your students. This equipment should be appropriate, safeguarded, and maintained during the program.

> **Safety boats and launches** should have proper U.S. Coast Guard and local licenses, as should their operators.
> **All boats and equipment,** whether owned by the program or by students, should be inspected daily and the results recorded on a Facility Inspection Form. If a boat is unsafe or lacks the proper equipment, you should not permit it to be used until the deficiencies are corrected.
> **Correct operation of a hoist should be taught** (if one is used) and its operation restricted to only those properly instructed in its use. A hoist should be inspected daily. Proper written and oral instruction concerning the use of any other equipment or procedures that sailors will use is also important.
> **Students should be taught responsibility** for their own equipment and respect for the property of others. You can help by providing secure storage areas for all boats, boat parts and

personal property. A rash of petty thefts that pit students (and parents) against each other and the instructors can be very debilitating to a program.

Many youth programs depend on volunteer parents or others to help transport students, and possibly boats and trailers, to distant regattas. Be sure that all **volunteer drivers** so involved are properly licensed and insured and that their towing equipment is appropriate.

6. Teach state-of-the-art methods.

Your instruction program should embody state-of-the-art teaching methods, incorporating US Sailing guidelines and your experience plus that of other instructional staff and the sponsoring organization. The sailing program should provide skill-level appropriate instruction as well as feedback. You should utilize resources such as *Learn Sailing Right!* that support US Sailing guidelines and are recognized as the "standard of excellence" in the sport of sailing.

Follow carefully the instruction plan you have drawn up, and make substitutions only with the approval of the sponsoring organization. Keep up with new sailing and teaching advances by reading current sailing publications, attending relevant symposiums and conferences and using newly-developed audio-visual tools that become available.

Proper instruction also presupposes careful selection of instructional staff and assurance that each staff member has been qualified.

Do all instructors have first aid and CPR training?
Are they certified by US Sailing?
Do they have the necessary required valid U.S. Coast Guard, state and automobile licenses?

7. Supervise activities carefully.

Supervision is a major responsibility, especially when younger students are involved. It begins before your students arrive at the sailing site and continues until after the last student has left for the day. At times it will require *General Supervision* and at other times it may require *Specific Supervision*. This supervision will include not only the students but also your staff A Program Director or Head Instructor has the overall responsibility even when he or she is not out on the water with a particular sailing class or near the activity in which they are engaged.

General supervision requires you to be in the area of the activity at all times to not only keep the program going but also to try to anticipate problems. *Specific supervision* of the sailors will be required at times when there is a higher risk of an injury. This might involve activities such as teaching a new sailing skill, conducting a swim test or responding to an emergency.

Supervision means maintaining a level of discipline appropriate to the activity. Hazing, raucous behavior and horseplay on or near the water can all lead to accidents and injury if not controlled. You certainly do not have to be a drill sergeant, but you must remain in control of activities. If a student is reprimanded or punished for inappropriate behavior, record the circumstances and discuss the situation with your sponsoring organization (and both parents if the student is a minor). Disruptive behavior can destroy both the fun and the learning process for other students, so prompt and effective action can be essential to the success of your program.

Consider also the recommended **instructor-to-student and safety-boat-to students-on-the-water ratios** when deciding on levels of supervision. One of the most frequent complaints in sports lawsuits involves the allegation of "failure to supervise." *The degree of supervision must be related to the degrees of potential risk.*

8: Prepare and test emergency procedures.

Emergencies can and will occur. You should **have <u>written procedures</u>** for a wide range of possible events, and you and your staff should TEST your ability to respond quickly and appropriately. (See the American Red Cross Emergency Action Plan (EAP) Recommendations earlier in this chapter, the Emergency Response Recommendations on the next page and the sample Emergency Form at the end of this section.) **Are you ready to handle:**

- a capsized boat?
- an overboard recovery?
- serious injury to a student (both at the dock and on the water)?
- a safety boat breakdown?
- the theft of critical equipment?
- a sudden change in weather conditions?

The real practice of risk management begins when you are forced to respond to an emergency, especially one in which several things go wrong at the same time.

Do you have the required first aid and CPR skills?
Can you communicate immediately from either land or water with professional emergency teams?
Do you know the emergency number for your area? (Not all areas have 911 systems in place.)
Do you know the location of, way to and distance to the nearest hospital emergency facilities?

The emergency plans that you prepare for a variety of risk scenarios should be reviewed carefully with your staff, your sponsoring organization and your local response team. These plans should be specific to your site and updated as appropriate.

EMERGENCY RESPONSE RECOMMENDATIONS...

IN AN EMERGENCY:

Call 911 (if applicable).

Call the appropriate agency(ies), i.e. Search & Rescue 555-714, Non-emergency Police 555766, or Non-emergency Sheriff 555742.

YOU SAY:

"This is an emergency. The telephone I am calling from is 1234567."

Exact nature of accident.
Medical assessment of victim.
Exact location of accident.

Description of victim and victim's name.
Your name.

Provide driving directions for emergency vehicle to get **to where the emergency is --** which may or may not be the facility's address. *Do not hang up until the operator has <u>hung up.</u>*

9: Maintain complete records of activities.

Each day an instructor should complete a **Log** (written record) of all sailing program activities, noting:

- weather and water conditions periodically, as well as significant changes Fit names of absent students
- incidents involving possible injury, physical damage or loss 0 conditions calling for repairs any other events of note

Each day the senior instructor should review and approve the Log, and each week's Logs should be reviewed by an appropriate supervisory authority. The Logs should be maintained as a permanent record. Should litigation occur, the Logs may be indispensable for defense.

Similarly, you should maintain in the records your **Emergency Action** Plan and any accident reports given to medical, police or insurance organizations. These records should also include any participation agreements, waivers, releases, or hold harmless agreements signed by students (or parents/guardians when applicable), student medical forms, progress reports on students, periodic facility inspection reports, and your daily/weekly lesson plans. (See sample forms at end of this section.)

10: Provide appropriate financing for risk.

Those sponsoring a sailing program should assure themselves, and their instructional staff, that adequate funds are available to meet the possible contingencies described in the risk assessment. This may mean the use of a special reserve fund or budget to cover the smaller losses that inevitably occur in any program. This also means provision of appropriate forms of insurance to protect the sponsoring organization, its employees, its members (if a club), its volunteers, and its instructional staff (if not employees). They should be protected from a variety of risks, including, but not limited to, physical damage to property, dishonesty and theft, legal liability, automobile liability, marine liability, workers' compensation, and the possibility of fines (if insurable). The details of this financing should be explained in full to the instructional staff so that they will understand their rights, duties and responsibilities, especially for insurance.

For example, if a sponsoring organization carries a deductible on its liability insurance policy that covers instructors, will that organization reimburse an instructor if he or she is sued and the deductible is imposed? Has the sponsoring organization provided proper workers' compensation protection, including Jones Act and comparable coverage? Has its automobile liability insurance been extended to cover non-owned vehicles, such as those used by instructors and volunteers? All of these areas of risk financing should be confirmed before starting a program. If your program supervisor does not include this information during staff training, ask!

The sponsoring organization can seek assistance from US Sailing and other specialists in determining what insurance may be appropriate and what limits of protection are prudent. Special insurance coverage is also available from programs endorsed by US Sailing for events such as regattas and through US Sailing for certified instructors. Specific details can be obtained from US Sailing.

Examples of Risk Management Situations

Each of the following cases involves risk, the chance that some future event may cause injury or harm to person or property. Each may also affect the success of your teaching program and the confidence that your sponsoring organization, students and their families have in your ability. Beyond that, a failure in judgment could mean a lawsuit and a black mark against the sport of sailing. If you have carefully followed the steps and responsibilities of risk management as outlined by this section, you will be able to answer the questions.

1) You are in your second year of teaching in Boston. Several of your returning sailors from last year's class want some early practice on a Saturday in late May. It's hot -- an uncharacteristic 90 degrees -- but you know the water temperature is still in the fifties. How do you advise these sailors?

Advise your students about the risks of hypothermia in the cold early spring waters off Boston and the importance of dressing appropriately, and you mandate that the sailors wear LIFE JACKETs and sail only when accompanied by a safety boat.

Boats are being readied for sailing off Washington's Bainbridge Island. It's slow at the hoist so one crew, with their boat fully rigged, decides to push their trailer to the other end of the grounds to launch at a ramp. What is your immediate concern?

Before allowing a crew to move their rigged boat to the launching ramp, you will check for overhead wires, determine whether the ramp is clean and free of debris, and provide proper supervision.

You're in the fourth week session at a summer camp in Louisiana. The heat is stifling and the humidity on the lake leaves you dripping with sweat. Ten doublehanded dinghies are setting out for a two-hour class. How should these sailors be prepared for the weather conditions?

Facing a day of high heat and humidity, your students should be wearing sun-protective gear and carrying plenty of liquids.

One of your students tells you she is missing $20 from the ditty bag she left on shore during class. How do you respond?

After an alleged theft, you will make a prompt investigation, report to students, parents (when applicable) and supervisors, and provide a secure place to store valuables in the future.

It's a typical hot, humid, and almost windless day on the Chesapeake Bay. Your sailors have almost completed their schedule of races, with only one short windward/leeward race remaining before calling it a day. Over on the western shore, however, a rising green-brown cloud mass foretells an afternoon squall, in which winds can reach 60 knots. Do you send your boats to the beach or try to get in the last race?

With a vicious squall imminent, you will send your students ashore to safety, well before the squall hits. Remember the motto, "When in doubt, don't go out!"

American Red Cross Emergency Action Plan (EAP) Recommendations

Developing an Emergency Action Plan

An EAP should be developed for any emergency that could occur in a small craft activity. An EAP includes these general features:

> How the person who recognizes the emergency is to signal others
> The steps each person in the group should take in an emergency
> The location of rescue and safety equipment
> Actions to minimize the emergency and safely rescue any victims
> How to call for medical assistance when needed
> Follow-up procedures after an emergency

Before writing your EAP, talk with fellow staff members, volunteer leaders, and participants. If you belong to an agency or organization, check its safety guidelines or consult with the safety officer.

Most emergency action plans include steps for managing specific types of emergencies. For example, an incident involving multiple victims may require coordinating the efforts of different group members.

Contents of an Emergency Action Plan

An emergency action plan should include the following content areas as appropriate:

Layout of facility/environment

Emergency Medical Services (EMS) access and entry/exit routes

Location of rescue and first aid equipment

Location of telephones, with emergency telephone numbers posted

Exits and evacuation routes

Equipment available

Rescue equipment

First aid supplies

Emergency equipment

Support personnel

Internal

> Staff members
> Volunteer leaders
> Participants

External

> EMS personnel (police officers and fire fighters)
> Search and rescue team and local Coast Guard
> Hospitals
> Staff Responsibilities

Assign each person or staff member a duty

> Provide care.
> Warn other craft of emergency.
> Meet EMS personnel.
> Interview witnesses

Communication

Means available to obtain medical help or access to call 9-1-1

> The local emergency number, and who will make the call • Chain of command
> Person to contact family/guardian
> Person to deal with media

Follow-up

> This includes such items as EAP evaluation and documentation. See the following section, "After an Emergency," for a detailed description of follow-up items.

After An Emergency

When an emergency is over, you may need to complete follow-up procedures. For example, you may be responsible for:

- Confirming that witnesses have been interviewed and their observations documented.
- Reporting the incident to the appropriate individual (this may be your supervisor) or authorities.
- Contacting a victim's family/guardian.
- Dealing with the media.
- Inspecting equipment and supplies used in the emergency. Make sure all equipment used is back in place and in good working condition. Replace any used supplies. • Filling out any report forms and transmitting the reports appropriately. • Conducting a debriefing or arranging a critical incident stress debriefing.
- Assessing what happened and evaluating the actions taken. You should
- Review the event as a group.
- Consider what worked well and what could have worked better.
- Change the EAP to correct any weak areas.
- Practice the new plan as soon as possible.

Reports

All injuries and incidents should be documented and reported appropriately. These reports may be used for insurance purposes and in a court of law. Some agencies or organizations may already have a form for this purpose. If not, one can be developed from the sample forms found at the end of this section.

Critical Incident Stress

An emergency involving a serious injury or death is a critical incident. The acute stress it causes an individual can overcome his or her ability to cope. This acute stress is called *critical incident stress.*

Some effects of critical incident stress may appear right away and others may appear after days, weeks, or even months have passed. People suffering from critical incident stress may not be able to perform their jobs well. If not managed properly, this acute stress may lead to a serious condition called post-traumatic stress disorder.

Signs of critical incident stress include the following:

- Confusion
- Lowered attention span; restlessness Denial
- Guilt or depression
- Anger
- Anxiety
- Changes in interaction with others
- Increased or decreased eating (weight gain or weight loss)
- Uncharacteristic, excessive humor or silence Unusual behavior
- Sleeplessness
- Nightmares

Critical incident stress requires professional help to prevent post-traumatic stress disorder. An individual can reduce stress by:

- Practicing relaxation techniques.
- Eating a balanced diet.
- Avoiding caffeine, alcohol, and drugs.
- Getting enough rest.
- Participating in some type of physical exercise or activity.

Critical Incident Stress Debriefing

A process called critical incident stress debriefing (CISD) brings together a group of people experiencing critical incident stress with some of their peers, such as other staff members, and a trained mental health professional. This process helps those with critical incident stress share and understand their feelings while learning to cope.

Emergency service agencies usually have CISD teams trained to respond and give critical incident stress debriefings. Emergency action plans should include information on obtaining help for managing critical incident stress.

For more information on CISD and stress management, contact: Critical Incident Stress Foundation, 10176 Baltimore National Pike, Suite 201, Ellicott City, Maryland 210423652, (410) 750 - 9600, or a local mental health professional.

Reprinted with permission of the American Red Cross

US Sailing Sailor Certification

In Appendix B is a checklist of 14 sailing skills required for US Sailing Small Boat Certification at two different wind ranges. Using US Sailing's Progressive Skills Recognition System (PSRS), you may begin earning immediate credit for the skills you have already learned. The system is self-pacing — you do not have to demonstrate all the listed skills at once.

Any currently certified US Sailing Small Boat Sailing Instructor may witness and verify listed skills by filling out and signing the appropriate wind range boxes. The verifying instructor must be US Sailing certified and personally observe the skill as it is performed.

You may certify at any or both wind speed ranges:

- Light Air (5-14 mph)
- Heavy Air (15+ mph)

You must satisfactorily pass all 14 skills in a wind range to be certified at that level. You receive credit automatically for any skill at a lower wind speed range by completing that skill requirement at a higher wind range. Once you have completed all of the skill requirements in any wind range, you are eligible for certification at that level. You may upgrade to a higher wind speed certification at any time be demonstrating sailing skills at the desired wind speed. Some skills have no wind speed requirement (for instance Knots/Lines) and need not be repeated for upgrades.

Each skill is separately evaluated on a simple pass/fail basis. Each boathandling maneuver must be performed satisfactorily in at least two out of three consecutive attempts. Every element in multi-part skills must be satisfied in order to pass that skill (no partial credits). Skills may be retested at any time, as many times as necessary. No coaching or assistance is permitted during testing.

When you have completed all of the skills in a given wind range and you are ready to apply for certification, make sure the book is filled out properly and mail it to US Sailing. US Sailing Membership is recommended but not required to obtain certification. If you are not already a US Sailing member, you may join when applying for certification.

SAILOR CERTIFICATION SYSTEM

SMALL BOAT SAILOR
For dinghies, keel and centerboard daysailers and catamarans

CERTIFICATION LEVELS:

- 4 Light Air (5-14 mph)
- 4 Heavy Air (15+ mph)

Small Boat Sailor Certification Record Book (or "Little Red Book")
The skills on the preceding page are outlined in the "Little Red Book (LRB)." They need to be verified by a US Sailing certified instructor, and some helpful hints to make this process easier follow.

First, if your curriculum includes all of the 14 skills listed in the LRB, and they are demonstrated to a certified instructor, you may simply sign the back page of the book on the Instructor Signature line beneath the words, "I attest the applicant has been properly tested on the skills signed off in this booklet." You can skip all the other entries and simply print your name, instructor number (which is your US Sailing membership number), and the job is done. You can do this by hand or use a rubber stamp.

Second, if any portion of your curriculum includes all the skills on a given page, and your student has demonstrated proficiency, you can sign off the entire page for a single wind speed range simply by signing at the top of the page. You can use your rubber stamp for this.

Third, if your students have demonstrated only some of the required skills, used a variety of boats, or a variety of wind ranges, you'll need to make all 5 entries in each skill box, so you'll definitely want to use rubber stamps for more than just signatures.

The Small Boat Sailor Certification Record Book provides a good curriculum outline and is a nice way for each student to document his or her progress. It also is a good "end-of-the-program" award.

Small Boat Racing Certification Record Book

This book offers 15 boathandling and racing skills, some at different wind ranges, which need to be verified by a US Sailing Small Boat Racing Level 2 Coach. It is one of the next possibilities that a sailor can pursue.

Other areas are the various levels of Keelboat Certification or the thrill of windsurfing.

The following Sailing Program samples have been taken from various programs across the United States to provide a greater representation of methods, techniques, and styles. Due to the range of the samples, the content information is not intended to flow or coincide from one example to the next.

SAMPLE: SYLLABUS

Basic Sailing Beginner

FORMAT: (8) three-hour lessons for youth or adults for one week or several weeks

TOPIC CLASS 1	TIME ALLOWANCE
Introduction and Course Overview	10 minutes
Team Building	15 minutes
Tour of Facility	15 minutes
Life Jackets - Inspection, Sizing and Lecture	10 minutes
Swim Test Lecture	5 minutes
Swim Test Actual Practical Test	30 minutes
Capsize Recovery	15 minutes
Capsize Recovery Practice	45 minutes
Basic Knots	30 minutes
Debrief	5 minutes

TOPIC CLASS 2	TIME ALLOWANCE
Introduction/ Review	15 minutes
Weather Lecture	20 minutes
Safe Sailing Lecture	15 minutes
Rigging Boats Demonstration	5 minutes
Rigging Boats Practice	25 minutes
First Sail Lecture	15 minutes
First Sail on the Water Practice	55 minutes
De-Rigging Boats	25 minutes
Debrief	5 minutes

TOPIC CLASS 3	TIME ALLOWANCE
Wind Lecture and Land Drills	5 minutes
Basic Sailing Maneuvers - Steering and Tacking	15 minutes
Rigging Boats	15 minutes
On the Water Practice	25 minutes
De-Rigging Boats	90 minutes
Weather Review	20 minutes
Debrief	5 minutes

TOPIC	CLASS 4	TIME ALLOWANCE
Introduction/Review		5 minutes
How a Sailboat Sails Lecture		10 minutes
Tacking Lecture and Land Drills		15 minutes
Rigging Boats		25 minutes
On the Water Practice		90 minutes
De-Rigging Boats		20 minutes
Knot Relay Race		10 minutes
Debrief		5 minutes

TOPIC	CLASS 5	TIME ALLOWANCE
Introduction/Review		10 minutes
Jibing Lecture and Land Drills		15 minutes
Rigging Boats		15 minutes
Hand Signals		10 minutes
On the Water Practice including Capsize Drill		90 minutes
De-Rigging Boats		15 minutes
Right-of-Way Lecture		20 minutes
Land Drill Debrief		5 minutes

TOPIC	CLASS 6	TIME ALLOWANCE
Introduction/Review		5 minutes
Steering Upwind and Use of Telltales		20 minutes
Rigging Boats		15 minutes
On the Water Practice		90 minutes
Docking Practice		30 minutes
De-Rigging Boats		15 minutes
Debrief		5 minutes

TOPIC	CLASS 7	TIME ALLOWANCE
Introduction/Review		5 minutes
Overboard Recovery Lecture, and Land Drills		30 minutes
Rigging Boats		15 minutes

On the Water Practice	90 minutes
De-Rigging Boats	15 minutes
Relay Race	20 minutes
Debrief	5 minutes

TOPIC CLASS 8	TIME ALLOWANCE
Introduction/Review	5 minutes
Rigging Boats	15 minutes
On the Water Practice	90 minutes
De-Rigging Boats	15 minutes
Review of Land Skills, Oral Review and Written Test	30 minutes
Debrief	5 minutes

SAMPLE: LESSON PLAN #1

Basic Sailing Beginner

LESSON PLAN FOR: Beginner   DATE: Monday

LESSON NUMBER: 1

OBJECTIVE/GOAL: basic knots, nomenclature, rig/derig, swim and scoop, acquaint students with basic knots, parts of the boats, rigging and de-rigging, scoop recovery and swim test

MATERIALS:

1 rigged 420

Class notebooks Lines for knot tying

CONTENT: Review: ---

1 de-rigged 420 1 safety boat

Material Introduction:

boat nomenclature, scoop recovery, and knots

Methods Activities:

(30 min.) Land Drill: basic knot demonstration and practice of bowline and figure-B

(40 min.) Land Demonstration: a) proper rigging of 420, b) de-rigging and proper storage of 420, c) scoop recovery

(40 min.) Water Drill: administer swim test and scoop recovery.

Students test two at a time, and then demonstrate scoop recovery on moored boat before getting out of water.

(40 min) Water Drill: students steering boat being towed - no sails. Each student takes turn as skipper and crew. Develop feel for stability and helm reaction.

Closure:

(20 min.) Review parts of the boat, and pass out nomenclature handout for notebooks.

REMARKS/COMMENTS

Students had full day with information overload. Towing worked well as a means of developing student comfort in the boats and increasing their confidence.

SAMPLE: LESSON PLAN #2

Basic Sailing Beginner

LESSON PLAN FOR: <u>Beginner 420</u> DATE: <u>Tuesday</u>

LESSON NUMBER: <u>2</u>

OBJECTIVE/GOAL: sailing on a reach

have students understand basic rigging of a 420 main & jib

students properly adjust sails and helm while sailing on a reach

students tack the boat in Figure-8 drill

MATERIALS:

Whiteboard & markers 3 de-rigged 420s

2 drop buoys 1 safety boat

CONTENT:

Review:

knots: bowline, Figure-8 parts of boat & sail

Material Introduction:

safety position, tacking & reaching for Figure-8 Water Drill

Methods Activities:

(20 min.) Chalk talk on: a) no-go zone for docking & stopping; b) tacking, reaching and Figure-8 Water Drill pattern; c) safety position if necessary on the water.

(30 min.) Practice for students as they rig boats.

(20 min.) Water Drill as students depart 420 float to immediate practice of the safety position.

(40 min.) Water Drill as students sail from practice of safety position drill to Figure-8 drill. Provide on-the-water coaching for sail adjustments and tacking practice.

(30 min) Practice for students as they de-rig the 420s making sure

Closure:

(20 min.) Review no-go zone and docking, body positions in boat, Figure-8 drill, safety position, and individual evaluations of strong points and areas for improvement.

REMARKS/COMMENTS

Sailing from boat float allowed for reaching in all segments of water drills. Figure-8 drill works well because it is a point and go pattern -- students just have to aim for the mark and push tiller towards sail.

SAMPLE: LESSON PLAN #3

Basic Sailing Beginner

LESSON PLAN FOR: Beginner 420 _____ DATE: Wednesday _____
LESSON NUMBER: 3 _____

OBJECTIVE/GOAL: reaching and sail adjustment
reinforce student confidence and comfort in the boat
reinforce proper body position and use of weight
continue practicing sail adjustment on reaches and tacking

MATERIALS:

Whiteboard & markers 3 de-rigged 420s
2 drop buoys   1 safety boat

CONTENT:

Review:

Safety position and tacking remind students of dangers from open automatic bailers during capsize recovery

Material Introduction:

new drill: Follow-the-Leader/safety boat

Methods Activities:

(15 min.) Chalk talk on: a) new water drill Follow-the-Leader that will emphasize sail adjustments to the wind, their course, and speed of their boats to maintain position in line. Emphasize no contact and tiller towards the trouble as a precaution.

(30 min.) Practice for students as they rig boats.

(40 min.) Water Drill as students practice Figure-8 Drill. Provide on-the-water coaching for sail adjustments and tacking practice.

(50 min.) Water Drill of students following the safety boat. Safety boat will drive in a pattern that causes students to sail from a close reach to a broad reach with some tacking. Provide some assistance regarding sail adjustments throughout the drill.

(20 min) Practice for students de-rigging the 420s making sure boats are secured and sails/equipment are properly stowed away.

Closure:

(20 min.) Review avoiding collisions. Provide some quizzing through Questions & Answers on scoop method, parts of boat and sail. Provide individual evaluations of strong paints and areas for improvement.

REMARKS/COMMENTS

Most of students grasp concepts introduced to date very well. Will be moving on to upwind sailing.

SAMPLE FORMS AND GUIDELINES

FORM 1 -- FACILITY INSPECTION GUIDELINES

PREMISES

1. Are exterior premises, including driveways, walkways, parking areas, ramps, docks, etc. in safe condition?

Are launch ramps of solid construction, offering good traction and adequate room for maneuvering?

Are the launching and staging areas free of overhead power line hazards?

Is a power hoist in use?

5. Is its operation restricted to staff?

Is the insured responsible for any piers, docks, or moorings?

Is so, are these properly arranged and maintained?

If located in tidal waters, is the design appropriate for changing water levels?

Is the space for sailing class well lighted and ventilated?

Is there a telephone and/or some means of contacting emergency help, if needed?

HOUSEKEEPING

Are facilities clean and well kept?

Is there proper trash storage and trash removal?

Are boats and equipment stored safely to prevent falling, vandalism, or theft and with adequate passageways for the equipment used to remove boats?

MAINTENANCE

1. Are facilities and equipment well maintained?

2. Is preventive maintenance done on a written schedule?

3. Are mechanical systems maintained by qualified persons?

I. Is an Emergency Action Plan posted?

Is there a First Aid kit available? If it is stored in a locked place, where is the key kept?

Is fire protection equipment provided?

Indicate which equipment is available:

Sprinklers

Extinguishers

Smoke or Heat Detection

Standpipe/Hose

Fire Alarm

Do the safety boat(s) have radios and required safety equipment? If it is not on the boat(s), where is it stored? If it is stored in a locked place, where is the key kept?

Is there a procedure for record keeping and inspections?

FORM 2 -- MEDICAL & EMERGENCY INFORMATION

(This form must be completed and signed by you or your parents (if you are a minor) and turned in prior to the start of your course.)

Name_____ Birth date_____ Gender_____

Address_____

      No.   Street   City   State   Zip

Do you have a history of or do you currently have, any physical limitations that might prevent you from fully participating in this course?   Yes   No

If yes, please specify missing or injured body parts, weakness, eyeglasses, contacts, hearing aids, etc.

_____

Do you have any learning differences that might prevent you from fully participating in this course?

Yes   No   If yes, please specify_____

Please check () those that apply and provide necessary information on reverse side of this form.

Chronic Ailments:

Asthma, or other respiratory problems Circulatory or heart problems

Diabetes or hypoglycemia

Epilepsy

Hemophilia, or other bleeding problems

Allergies:

Insect bites

Bee stings

Foods Drugs

Others, if significant

Current medications or pertinent information

Blood type_____   Date of last tetanus shot_____

Family physician name _____Phone_____

Date of most recent physical examination_____

Where are your medical records kept?_____

Insurance Carrier_____   Insurance ID _____

Who should be notified in case of emergency?

Name_____   Relation_____

Phone (C)_____   (R)_____

Name_____   Relation_____

Phone (C)_____   (R)_____

I, the undersigned, do hereby authorize and consent to any x-ray examination, anesthetic, medical or surgical diagnosis or procedure rendered under the general or specific supervision of any member of the medical staff or of a dentist licensed under the provisions of the Education Law and/or Public Health Law of the State of_____and on the staff of any hospital holding a current operating certificate issued by the Department of Health of the State of_____. It is understood that this authorization is given in advance of any specific diagnosis, treatment or hospital care being required but is given to provide authority and power to render care which the aforementioned physician in the exercise of his/her best judgment may deem advisable. It is understood that effort shall be made to contact the above people prior to rendering treatment to the patient, but that any of the above treatment will not be withheld if any of these people cannot be reached.

Signature_____

Name (please print)_____

Date_____
 Applicant, or Parent/Guardian (if a minor)

FORM 3 -- EMERGENCY PROCEDURE

In the event of an emergency or incident, the *DUTY MANAGER will:*

GET HELP

FIRE:

• Get people and staff out of the area • Ca11911

INJURY:

• Provide immediate first aid • Ca11<u>911</u>

• Disburse onlookers

INCIDENT:

Robbery, obnoxious customer, collision (boat/car), trespasser, stolen property/boat

• Call Police at

For less serious incidents (i.e., Coast Guard/Harbor Police stop, private boat unaccounted for, etc.)

• Contact <u>Marina Supervisor</u>

LOST RENTAL BOAT:

• Make sure all boats are accounted for at closing time.

• Search for boats before dark (all boats should be in sight one hour before closing) and take a VHF radio

• Have the office attendant monitor channel 68

• If boat cannot be found, call <u>Harbor Police at</u>

THEN CALL Manager

Assistant Manager Office Supervisor

The above will contact or (if the Duty Manager is unable to reach one of the above supervisors) the *DUTY MANAGER will* report to:

Assistant Director

Director

Owner

The Owner is to be notified at   in the event of fire, serious injuries, and incidents requiring assistance from other law enforcement or emergency response agencies.

Accidents, injuries, and incidents MUST be reported in writing as soon as possible after their occurrence to the Marina Manager. Reports will be submitted no later than the end of the shift following the incident

FORM 4 -- PARTICIPATION AGREEMENT

The Basic Sailing course you are about to begin is an exciting and demanding challenge. but you need to be aware of what will be involved and be willing to study and practice to achieve success.

A swim test is required of all students, which consists of swimming 50 yards in the waters of the area you will be sailing in, in sailing clothing and footwear. The attached student registration and medical and emergency information form must be completed and signed by you or your parents (if you are a minor) and turned in no later than

You will be required to provide a life jacket (vest type) which should be Coast Guard approved, the proper size for your weight and build, and be form fitting and comfortable, as you will be wearing it at all times during the course. Put your name on it with waterproof ink. Proper footwear will also be worn at all times, both on land and on the water. Bring a change of clothes, a towel, a lined notebook for note taking, two pencils, and a waterproof felt tip pen to each lesson.

The fee for this course is   . Your instructor will be

Lessons begin on   , starting at   AM / PM and ending at   AM / PM.

I understand that in entering this sailing course I agree to obey all program rules as set forth by the program director and the instructors, that I will use utmost care in the use of the boats and equipment, that I will not engage in any horseplay or other disruptive behavior. I understand that failure to attend regularly, arrive promptly, abide by the rules may result in my suspension from the program.

Applicant's Signature_____   Date_____

I assume full responsibility for any loss or damage, excepting loss or damage covered by insurance, that may come to any person. boat, sailboard, equipment, pier, float, or other property used in conjunction with this course as the result of improper use, negligence, violation of the rules, and other acts of sailors, or other representatives of the school, instructional program or host location in connection herewith. I accept that the sport of sailing and the conduct of this course entail and are subject to certain inherent risks and assume all risks on land and on the water of participation in this program. I further agree to hold the school, instructional program or host location, US Sailing, and their representatives harmless for personal injuries and/or property damage.

Signature_____   Date_____
Applicant, or Parent/Guardian (if a minor)

Parental/Guardian Agreement (if student is a minor):

I understand the contents of this statement and agree to see to it that my kid adheres to the program rules. I agree to assume the obligation for the expenses of repair and/or replacement of program equipment that is attributable to my kid's reckless or irresponsible behavior. I agree to make an appointment for a parent-instructor conference if requested.

Parent/Guardian's Signature_____   Date_____

FORM 5 -- INJURY REPORT

No._____   Street_____

INJURED: Person Address_____

Phone_____

Age_____   Gender_____

_____

City   State   Zip

(B)_____   (R)_____

Association with program **INJURY:**

Describe injury

Where taken

Name of Physician/Hospital Physician's diagnosis

First Aid administered by Time First Aid administered **ACCIDENT:**

Date   Time

Address

Exact location at address

Describe accident

AM / PM

AM/PM

City   State   Zip

Names, addresses, and telephone numbers of witnesses:

List below: weather conditions; water conditions; water temperature; air temperature; tide conditions; boat and equipment particulars.

Draw diagram below if a collision was involved.

Report prepared by   Date

Signature

Reviewed by   Date

Signature

Corrective measures

Date person returned to program

Restrictions on activities

FORM 6 -- STUDENT REGISTRATION

POLICY GUIDELINES

As a sailing instructor or administrator of a program it is important to develop site-specific policies which will handle day to day administration needs and emergency situations. Listed below are some subjects that should be considered if teaching or administering a sailing program.

Emergency Procedures for:

- Injury
- Overboard Recovery
- Sailboat recovery
- Powerboat recovery
- Vessel collision with possibility of sinking
- Grounding
- Fire (afloat and ashore)
- Weather change (squall or thunderstorm)
- Record Keeping Procedures
- Student Discipline
- Student Dissatisfaction
- Broken Equipment
- Radio Use
- Life Jacket Use
- Non-Emergency Medical Transportation or Admission
- Non-Injury Vessel Collision and Property Damage
- Employee Personal Equipment Use
- Launching/Hoist Usage
- Insurance
- Property
- Medical

RECORD KEEPING GUIDELINES

Instructors and administrators have a responsibility to keep accurate written records. A thorough program should include the following.

1. Medical Forms
2. Permission/Waivers
3. Participation Agreements
4. Registration Forms
5. Swim Test Records
6. Attendance Records
7. Daily Log
8. Weather
9. Unusual Items
10. Lesson Plans
11. Program Schedules
12. Student Lists
13. Student Certification Awards
14. Course Evaluations
15. Equipment List/Inventories
16. Equipment Order Forms
17. Broken Equipment Forms
18. Accident Report Forms
19. Job Descriptions
20. Employee Discipline
21. Time Sheets
22. Mailing Lists
23. Publicity/Marketing Forms

Providing Leadership, Integrity and Advancement for the sport of sailing in the United States

US Sailing was originally organized as the North American Yacht Racing Union (NAYRU) on October 30, 1897. As the National Governing Body for the sport of sailing the organization works to achieve its mission through a wide range of programs and services geared towards promoting participation in sailing and providing a level playing field for all sailors.

US Sailing sets the course for sailors to enjoy the sport for a lifetime. For those just beginning, US Sailing ensures that they will learn from experienced and certified instructors who are trained using a national standards and an acclaimed curriculum. For sailing programs and one-design sailing organizations, US Sailing's National Sailing Programs and One-Design Sailing Symposiums bring together experts who address the latest developments in these fields of the sport. Young sailors just starting out in the sport can learn about sailboat racing through one of many Junior Olympic sailing festivals organized by US Sailing every year.

For racing sailors, US Sailing ensures integrity on the course and a level playing field by training and certifying race officials, judges, and umpires and by maintaining standardized rules and sailing instructions. The 18 National Championships organized by US Sailing offer various disciplines of racing where sailors test their skills against the best in the country. US Sailing provides handicap rating certificates and safety programs for sailboat owners who enjoy competing in offshore events. For sailors aiming to represent the USA at the Olympic and Paralympic Games, US Sailing trains, selects, and manages the national sailing team, US Sailing Team Sperry Top-Sider.

Visit us to learn more at ussailing.org.

NOTES

NOTES

NOTES